The Values Advantage

The Foundation for Leading with a Clear Purpose

Wes Dove

DOVE DEVELOPMENT & CONSULTING

HARNESSING THE POWER OF THE VALUES ADVANTAGE

"When we stopped posting values and started living them, our veteran employment program soared from the high 40s to the top 10 nationwide—proof that true transformation begins with the heart."
LTC (Ret) Dr. Robert M Walker, Jr., Director of Workforce Services Operations, Virginia Employment Commission

"Identifying core values unlocked transformative potential, clarifying our purpose and enabling us to lead with intention, inspire our community, and create an environment where survivors feel safe, seen, and empowered."
Sabrina Dorman-Andrews, Co-Founder/Executive Director of New Creation VA

"Once we made our values explicit, gave them a champion, and wove them into reviews and weekly conversations, they stopped being words on a wall and became the daily operating system of our company."
Gil Colman, Founder of Colman Engineering

"When CASCADE became the way we actually operate under pressure, not just words on a slide, clients stayed, teams delivered miracles, and choosing the right thing, even when it's harder, became our competitive edge."
Jorge Velasco, President/CEO of BR Printers

"When you shine a light on values lived out loud, they multiply. Recognition becomes more than applause—it becomes a strategy for leading with values every day."
Crystal Farmer, Sr. VP/COO of Augusta Health

"When every decision flows from clear, community-first values (P.R.I.D.E.), officers run toward danger, excellence becomes intentional, and an entire department lives the oath we swore—protecting and serving with heart."
Phillip Read, Chief of Police for Bridgewater, VA

"When leaders truly embody Integrity, Caring, Innovation, Teamwork, and Excellence every day, values stop being slogans and become the lived behaviors that turn clients into partners and teams into high-performing families."
Larry Cain, District Manager with Insperity

"Clear core values give us our identity; a strong culture puts those values into daily action—so the people in the big red truck and the people in our community are truly connected heart-to-heart."
Ben Coffman, Deputy Fire Chief/Emergency Management Coordinator for Frederick Co., VA

"When our core values were just words on a wall, we decided to make them the heartbeat of Pioneer Bank again; and everything changed."
Josh Hale, Senior VP/Market President with Pioneer Bank

"When the majority of the team finally shares the same values, challenges become opportunities, breakeven projects become money-makers, customers become fans, and employees become true partners."
Jordan Rohrer, President of The Power Connection

"After eighty-four years, the fuels have changed, but the promise hasn't: our five values aren't on a poster—they're in every tank, every call, every handshake."
Josh Stephens, General Manager, Rockingham Petroleum Cooperative

The Values Advantage
The Foundation for Leading with a Clear Purpose

Published by Dove Development & Consulting, LLC, Rockingham, VA
www.dove-development.net

This publication is designed to provide accurate and authoritative information with regard to the subject matter covered. It is sold with the understanding that the publisher and author are not engaged in rendering legal, accounting, psychological, or other professional advice. If legal advice or other expert assistance is required, the service of a competent professional should be sought.

ISBN 979-8-9920436-3-1 (paperback)
ISBN 979-8-9920436-4-8 (hardback)
ISBN 979-8-9920436-5-5 (ebook)
ISBN 979-8-9920436-6-2 (audio)

Cover design: Wes Dove

First Edition

Learn More at www.tva-framework.com

CONTENTS

FOREWORD

When Wes Dove approached me about writing the foreword to his third book, *The Values Advantage*, I was honored and intrigued. I can remember from a very young age my parents, both extremely ethical and hard-working, reinforcing the importance of values and that abiding by such values would serve as a strong foundation as I grew older.

Having spent 30 years in Corporate America, most recently as Chairman, President, and CEO of a super-regional insurance company operating in 19 states with almost $1 billion in revenue and $2 billion in assets, I remembered the message taught to me by my parents 50 years earlier. Values matter! The investment necessary to ensure that our teammates understood the company's values, which I refer to as the "DNA" of our company from which all of our decisions are based, was substantial though worth the effort. As our teammates became more comfortable operating in an environment where values were openly shared, discussed, and adherence evaluated as a critical component of performance reviews, buy-in grew exponentially as well as results! Revenue doubled and profitability tripled over a six-year period and even more impressive was that 98% of teammates surveyed planned to stay with the company over the next five years!

In mid-2021, our family moved to Virginia to be closer to aging parents and it was during this time I met Wes and Cindy Dove. My wife and I were very interested in purchasing a family business and had evaluated a number of opportunities before finalizing a deal to acquire the Waynesboro Landscape & Garden Center located in Waynesboro, Virginia. The former owners introduced me to their accountant who also had worked with Wes and Cindy in the past and he made the connection. We met at the Harrisonburg, Virginia Sub Station Mexican Grill!

Our conversation went smoothly and my wife Kim and I found Wes and Cindy very engaging and warm. We outlined our thoughts for our newly acquired family business and listened as Wes and Cindy discussed their capabilities and how potentially we could partner together. Wes had mentioned that they were licensed trainers of John Maxwell's leadership methodologies and practices which struck a chord immediately. Just a few years before, John Maxwell served as our keynote speaker during my former company's 60-year anniversary and I was able to share the stage as well as a Maxwell Minute with him, one of the highlights of my career! To find someone, or a pair of someone's who were greater disciples of John Maxwell's leadership philosophy than me at the Sub Station Mexican Grill was inspirational.

In the 75-year history of the Waynesboro Landscape & Garden Center, never was a mission statement, handbook, or set of values ever documented. In addition, it was quite apparent that the former owners made the majority, if not all, of the decisions. While performing due diligence on this 75-year-old family business, the former owners were gracious to allow Kim and I the opportunity to meet with several of the key people in both the landscape and garden center operations. Prior to actually acquiring the business, we were having in-depth discussions regarding values, the "non-negotiables", the guidepost of the business. While neither Kim or I had any prior landscape or garden center experience, we did know that having a company rooted in values would afford us the opportunity to attract and retain talent, make more informed decisions, and establish trust and buy-in of existing as well as new teammates. Collectively we agreed on 5 values: family, dependability, integrity, compassion, and humility. If you are part of the Garden Center operation, visibility has recently been added as a value (based on subjective evaluation only, we estimate that being visible with customers and proactively engaging in a warm and sincere approach, generates 5-10% additional revenue per transaction).

Wes diligently (and painfully) partnered with me to draft a Handbook and finalize our Mission Statement which we then presented throughout our company. While important, these pale in comparison to the foundational values that serve as the lifeblood of our business. One of our teammates artfully drafted a picture of a tree with each of our 5 values as branches which have been imprinted on the back of our company shirts. A moment that Wes and I will never forget is when one of our senior leaders elicited an emotional response which underscored the impact of values that aligned with his life's work yet had been absent! Moreover, there is no doubt that the emphasis, focus, and consistent presence of values in our daily dialogue helped to retain 100% of the key teammates after acquisition.

As I read Wes's new book, *The Values Advantage*, he clearly makes the case for values-driven leadership. A company that does NOT have clearly defined values where each teammate understands specifically what each value means and how to put into practice on a daily basis inevitably will suffer from disengagement, higher turnover, and ambiguity when it comes to making decisions. These higher costs can paralyze a business if not end the business!

Wes articulates that everyone who comes into contact with your business cares about the values on display: teammates, customers, vendor partners, and the community at large. The tone starts at the top with the most senior leaders in your organization consistently leading by example! Our teammates witness me and other top leaders picking up trash, watering plants, and taking a customer's cart to and from their vehicle. How can you have a value of Humility if the owners and those in high positions of authority are not willing to "walk the talk?"

Wes's insights and practical advice on how to make values a competitive advantage that have a lasting impact are often overlooked in business today. I strongly encourage you to reflect upon the insight and wisdom contained within these pages and to put into practice a framework of values that guide your journey.

Craig Johnson
Owner and Vice President
Waynesboro Landscape & Garden Center, Virginia Boxwood Company,
and All Seasons Irrigation & Lighting

INTRODUCTION

For more than two decades of working alongside John Maxwell, one truth has proven itself time and time again: leadership makes the difference. I've seen it in businesses and governments, in nonprofits and community organizations. No matter the size or structure, leadership determines whether a team thrives or simply survives.

John defines leadership as *influence—nothing more, nothing less*. That definition has guided my life and my work. But here's what I've learned: influence isn't given because of a title, a position, or a corner office. It's earned—through consistent action rooted in something deeper: values.

That's why I'm excited about *The Values Advantage: The Foundation for Leading with a Clear Purpose*. Wes Dove has written a timely and practical guide that shows why values are the true foundation of leadership—and how they drive results you can measure.

At Maxwell Leadership, we've built everything we do around six core values: People, Growth, Passion, Leadership, Performance, and Transformation. These aren't slogans— they're the standards that shape how we lead, serve, and add value to others. When I met Wes and Cindy Dove in 2015, I quickly saw they lived by these same values. As members of our President's Advisory Council, they've given countless hours equipping leaders to apply these principles where they matter most—in the real world.

Wes's background gives him a rare combination of credibility and clarity. With more than 25 years in safety, human resources, and leadership development—spanning manufacturing, mining, and construction—he's seen the direct connection between values and performance. In *The Values Advantage*, he doesn't just tell you why values matter; he shows you how to build them into the DNA of your culture.

One of the biggest myths I encounter in leadership is that values are "soft." That couldn't be further from the truth. In every country I've visited with John, I've seen organizations fail not because of poor strategy or limited resources, but because their leaders lost sight of their values. The best leaders—the ones who build trust, loyalty, and longevity—are the ones who live out their core values every day.

Wes understands this from experience. Years ago, he left a stable, well-paying position because he couldn't reconcile his company's stated values with the behaviors of its leaders. That decision became the turning point of his career. Since then, he and Cindy have helped organizations across industries anchor their cultures in values—and the results speak for themselves. One example Wes shares in this book is a company led by Craig and Kim, who reduced voluntary turnover to just 5% over two years—compared to an industry average of 25%, according to the Bureau of Labor Statistics—by consistently modeling their core values. That's the kind of measurable impact that values can deliver, and it's why this book is so timely.

This book unfolds in three clear sections. The first, *The Case for Values-Driven Leadership*, helps you understand why values aren't optional—they're essential. The second, *Practical Applications for Building a Values-Based Culture*, equips you with tools to put those values to work every day. And the third, *A Framework for Lasting Impact*, shows you how to make those values stick—so they drive growth, performance, and transformation for years to come.

What I appreciate most about Wes's approach is that it mirrors our own belief at Maxwell Leadership: growth isn't accidental—it's intentional. You'll find no flu< here. Every chapter is filled with real stories, practical systems, and proven results.

So, as you read *The Values Advantage*, I challenge you to pause and reflect on your own leadership. Are your values visible in your daily actions? Do your team and clients see them in how you serve, decide, and lead?

Because here's the truth—leadership is influence, and influence starts with values.

This book will help you strengthen that foundation. And when you do, you'll not only lead better—you'll live better, too.

Mark Cole
CEO, Maxwell Leadership

PROLOGUE

When I think of Wes Dove, one word always comes to mind: *values*. Not the kind of values that get framed and hung on an office wall, or tucked into a handbook that no one reads again, but the kind that are lived out day after day, in quiet, consistent ways that shape people and leave a legacy.

I've had the privilege of watching Wes and his wife and business partner, Cindy, lead with their values long before this book ever existed. And the truth is, the stories I've witnessed are exactly why this book matters so much for leaders today.

Living Values Behind the Scenes

Years ago, when I was serving as Event Producer for Maxwell Leadership, the role carried enormous responsibility. Thousands of leaders came together at those events with high expectations—every detail needed to reflect excellence, every moving part needed to be coordinated with precision, and the weight of John Maxwell's legacy was always at the forefront. It was exhilarating work, but also demanding.

In the middle of that, Wes and Cindy showed up—not to take the spotlight, not to promote themselves, but to serve. They volunteered their time, energy, and expertise, stepping into the gaps that no one else saw but that mattered deeply to the success of the event.

I remember watching them work. While others rushed about, Wes and Cindy carried themselves with calm, steady presence. They modeled what it looks like to value people first, lending a helping hand and making sure I was "good". Their attitude wasn't "we have to do this" but "we get to serve here." And it wasn't lost on me.

That experience has stayed with me because it reminded me that leadership isn't about the microphone or the title. It's about how you choose to live your values when no one is applauding. Wes and Cindy demonstrated that the truest form of leadership is service, and that values are the foundation that make such service possible.

Building a Culture of Legacy

Fast forward to 2025, and I saw Wes and Cindy leading in an entirely different way—but with the same values. They hosted the *2025 LeadershipLegacy Experience*, and I had the honor of being a guest panelist.

From the moment I walked in, I knew this was not just another leadership conference. It had a different atmosphere. People weren't just there to collect information—they were part of something that felt purposeful, personal, and transformative. That didn't happen by accident. It was the direct result of the culture Wes and Cindy created.

Every detail of that event reflected who they are and what they stand for. The way they honored their clients. The way they empowered emerging leaders to share their stories. The way they fostered a spirit of community where everyone—from panelists to participants—felt seen and valued.

It was more than an event. It was a living demonstration of what happens when leaders build on values. Attendees walked away with more than notes in a journal; they left with a deeper sense of clarity about who they wanted to be and how they wanted to lead.

For me, it was a full-circle moment. Years earlier I had seen Wes and Cindy serving behind the scenes. Now I saw them building a stage for others, lifting leaders higher, and modeling the truth that values aren't just personal—they're contagious. They shape teams, clients, and communities.

Why This Book Matters

The stories you're about to read in this book are filled with principles and practices, but here's what makes them different: they aren't theory. They are rooted in lived experience. Wes has spent his career not just studying leadership, but living it—in businesses, in communities, and alongside leaders who have discovered that values are the only foundation that lasts.

What you'll find in these pages is a clear framework for understanding, defining, and living your values. You'll see why values are not just words but commitments that shape decisions, lead culture, and build reputations that stand the test of time. You'll also see the contrast: what happens when values are ignored, sidelined, or reduced to slogans.

And you won't just hear from Wes. Throughout this book, you'll encounter stories from leaders across industries who have learned what it means to align their work and their lives with values. Their stories—raw, practical, and inspiring—prove that the principles you're about to read can create real results in the real world.

An Invitation

As you turn these pages, I want you to do more than absorb information. I want you to imagine yourself in the stories. Ask yourself: *What do I value most? Am I living those values in my leadership, or just speaking them? Do the people around me experience those values in action?*

Because here's the truth: the leaders you're about to learn from are not superheroes. They are ordinary people who made extraordinary commitments. They decided that their values would not be negotiable, and that decision changed everything—their teams, their clients, their organizations, and their legacies.

That same decision is available to you.

Wes and Cindy's lives remind me that leading with values isn't about perfection—it's about intentionality. It's about showing up consistently, serving faithfully, and creating cultures where people know what matters most. And the beauty is, you don't have to wait for a stage or a title to begin. You can start living your values today, right where you are.

So lean in. This book is not just about leadership—it's about life. It's about discovering your own *Values Advantage* and using it to build something that lasts.

And if you'll allow it, the lessons that follow will challenge you, inspire you, and equip you to lead with clarity, conviction, and courage.

That's the power of values. That's the invitation of this book. And that is the legacy Wes Dove is handing to you.

Lane Jones
Chief Entrepreneurial Officer
Jones Lane Branding & Marketing

SECTION ONE

THE CASE FOR VALUES-DRIVEN LEADERSHIP

Core values are the heartbeat of any thriving organization, and this section makes the case for why they matter. Through personal stories, Chapters 1–6 reveal how values shape team engagement, client trust, and organizational reputation. Contrasting successes with high-profile failures, these chapters expose the costs of neglecting values and the rewards of living them out. From employee buy-in to community impact, the narrative underscores the truth that values are not just words but the foundation for sustainable success.

Exploring these chapters, you'll see why aligning behaviors with clear values is critical for any leader aiming to build a lasting legacy. This sets the stage for practical applications in subsequent sections.

CHAPTER ONE

VALUES: THE FOUNDATION FOR EVERY ORGANIZATION

In 2012, I made my first significant career change in more than a decade. While I had a hand in various human resource tasks and projects during the dozen or so years I led our facility's behavior-based safety process—and supported many of our company's locations across North America that were active in that same initiative—this move pulled me c«ompletely away for safety and landed me neck deep into a world I previously only thought I understood. As I wrapped up *Leading With a Clear Purpose*[1], I shared how my purpose evolved. I had found tremendous fulfillment in being able to pass along some of the tools I'd learned to use as I advanced in my own career, and see my peers earn similar opportunities for advancement as a result. It seemed like moving into a role where my complete focus would be on our "human resources" was the next logical step.

What I experienced during the next two years or so was anything but that! I could look across the hall into my former office, but that's as close as I got to feeling the kind of purpose I had been able to draw from developing the folks I worked with through that behavior-based safety process. I typically arrived at my office before 6 am, initially to have some undistracted time to focus on the college courses I was taking (with the hope of avoiding jail for violating some sort of employment law). It didn't take long for the folks whose shift began at 6:30 am to realize they could catch me with any issues they had before their day started, and the folks whose shift ended at the same time discovered they had a chance to bend my ear on their way out.

By the time I worked through all that each day, the rest of the office staff had started rolling in, and it was time for me to dive into my daily routine of working through time and attendance issues, internal or external interviews to fill open positions, or address any disciplinary matters that needed my attention. All of them, of course, ended up needing my attention.

Since I shared it in detail in both *What's KILLING Your Profitability? (It ALL Boils Down to Leadership!)*[2] and *Leading With a Clear Purpose*, I'll only mention it briefly again now for perspective. During the final eighteen months I worked in that role, I hired 225 external candidates and led interview teams to fill what felt like at least half that many positions with internal candidates. This only accounted for around half the time I was in the building. Throughout the last year and a half, I rarely left my office before 6:30, and I recall walking out on numerous evenings between 7:30 and 8 pm. Had that been where it stopped— from 6 am to 6:30 pm—Monday through Friday, it wouldn't have been much different from what I've seen most salaried employees juggle routinely, or what Cindy and I had been doing for our entire married life between our regular jobs and any side projects we had going.

But it most certainly did not stop there! Phone calls through the night and on the weekends became far too normal. Carrying a laptop home on holidays, or with me whenever we left town for a few days, was almost mandatory to avoid falling behind.

At the risk of sounding arrogant, I had become highly effective at keeping all the proverbial plates spinning. The workload itself wasn't all that bad; it just sucked up a lot of time. The most challenging part of it all, and what played a significant role in my deciding to leave that organization after working there for what was then my entire adult life, was constantly hiring people to work for a management team that I no longer believed lived up to the core values detailed in our employee handbook. The same handbook I had invested countless hours into producing the most recent revision.

Don't mistake any of this for me attacking that organization, for making me work too hard or having devious intentions. I have yet to find a way to excel in any role that carries even the slightest bit of leadership responsibility without putting in more than a 40-hour week. And while the company as a whole had indeed changed quite a bit over the nearly two decades I had been there, I can't point to anyone at the executive level who had horns or carried a pitchfork. Looking back, I'm convinced that the deciding factor boiled down to no longer seeing where the things I valued most were valued by the people I reported directly to. As difficult as the decision was, I realized that it was time for a change.

Good Organizations, But Something Was Missing

On October 6, 2014, I started working for a new organization for the first time since I was 19 years old. Truth be told, I thought I would spend the rest of my career there. I was doing similar work to what I had done in manufacturing, but this was for a family-owned business with just under fifty employees. My manager was the son of one of the owners and a fantastic person. The work in that particular industry carried some significant risks, but it was nothing short of fascinating. To top it all off, I quickly realized how much most of the management team truly cared about each individual working there.

I was responsible for developing a handbook, which may have been the first in the company's history (although I'm not entirely sure about that), processing payroll, filling open positions, onboarding new team members, and assisting with performance appraisals and any disciplinary conversations. Since completing those tasks for a company with fewer than fifty employees took substantially less time than what I had just left at a site with close to 650, I also jumped in to help with the company's safety initiatives whenever I could. Working 7 am to 5 pm, Monday through Friday, in an actual Monday-to-Friday role, was like having a part-time job in comparison—and that's actually what led Cindy to push me toward starting our business a few months later. However, we'll revisit that later on.

As much as I liked the company, and as great as most of the management team was, I couldn't say I was overly familiar with a core set of values that guided everyone's work. I'm not suggesting that they were doing anything wrong; I'm just sharing that I couldn't point to a solid *reason* behind what we did.

> **I'm not suggesting that they were doing anything wrong; I'm just sharing that I couldn't point to a solid *reason* behind what we did.**

About a year into what I thought would be the last job of my career, an opportunity found me. I was offered the chance to serve as the Safety & Human Resources Manager for another family-owned business, but it was in the construction field I had started before I even had a driver's license. Still doing work very similar to what I had done for the previous decade and a half, the workload was manageable even though I was juggling both responsibilities and, for now, nearly 100 employees. Again, I enjoyed the industry, and I respected the majority of my coworkers.

Before you interpret either of those references about "most of the management team" being great or "respected the majority of my coworkers" as me making a negative statement about those companies, I challenge you to name any group or organization where you've had a perfect relationship with every single person. In more than three decades in the working world, I've learned that the folks who say they get along with everyone all the time will likely lie about other things, too!

As in my previous two roles, I helped that organization write a handbook. In this case, we only released a revised edition, but it contained some significant changes. Like each of the other handbooks I had worked on for the other two companies, this one had a few pages early on dedicated to the organization's specific mission, vision, and values. While I recall those being included, I don't remember anything specific about them, nor much about the ones from the other companies. Not even the one I had worked at for nearly twenty years.

Overall, I enjoyed many aspects of my roles and appreciated the working relationships I had with most of my peers. However, I couldn't say that I truly loved any of those companies, mainly because I'm not entirely sure my values aligned with theirs. This is not to say they didn't have values, just to say that I couldn't tell what theirs were. If I heard them at any point, it was only in passing, not nearly enough to develop a clear picture as to what such values looked like in practice, or how they aligned with the work I was doing.

Since moving into full-time self-employment, I've helped numerous companies with safety and human resource-related tasks, though that's not what I find fulfilling at this point, or where we've dedicated our focus. Each time I've worked on a handbook, helped with staffing, or even had a hand in safety meetings with the employees in those organizations, there's almost always been some sort of reference to the company's mission, vision, or values. Rarely have I heard more than a vague reference. Interestingly enough, the places where I've heard values discussed more frequently, and in more detail, have also become some of our favorite organizations to work with. That's not a coincidence!

Identifying What Was Missing...

As I opened the second part of Leading With a Clear Purpose, I made a strong case for how much each of us is attracted to being part of something that matters. I'm convinced that this applies to everyone, regardless of their level within any organization. There are plenty of folks who do what they do, day in and day out, without having committed to a definite purpose, but I'd bet just about all of them would change that quickly if given the chance.

Just like with the companies I worked for as an employee, Cindy and I have found that some of the organizations we serve through our business are a better fit than others. As we began—especially early on, and during the lean times forced upon us by the COVID shutdowns—we were willing to do nearly anything we were capable of for almost anyone willing to pay us. For the most part, though, we did get to work with people we liked. But even then, there were times when things went as smoothly as we could have hoped, and times when it was just tough. By "tough", I don't mean the actual work itself, rather landing on what the outcome should look like, or what further steps were necessary to get there.

> **There were times when things went as smoothly as we could have hoped, and times when it was just tough.**

In many of the most challenging cases, we received pushback on what we needed to charge—be that for a complete package or a set hourly rate—precisely because so much organizational legwork was invisible, unbillable and thus harder to quantify.

Don't throw stones at me here. Our founding goal has always been to provide an exponential return on investment through anything we do. Quite honestly, there have been several occasions where the proposal we submitted was brushed aside because it was too *low*. I realize you may not believe that; hell, it's dumbfounded me every single time. But I can point to at least a half dozen specific examples.

Not long ago, we had the opportunity to chat with an executive from a company for which we had done extensive work, just after he retired. I asked him how we compared to what he had expected when initially contracting with us. He shared that our price point was about 50% of what he thought we'd charge, and we'd delivered better than anyone he'd ever worked with. As strange as it sounds, far too many folks in a role like his will see a price point that low and assume it subpar. We've had to work on that, whether we've wanted to or not.

The common theme we've found through our work over the last decade is that the organizations we've worked with most effectively have also been those that share our most common values. And while we didn't necessarily connect it directly to those shared values initially, it has certainly stood out more and more as time has gone by. Specific to our business relationships, these scenarios have also been instances where cost is rarely part of the conversation—mainly because the value we produce with them through the end result has been what we've all been focused on. Interestingly enough, we've experienced the same thing in relationships with boards, associations, and even friends. When we've placed like value on similar things, we experience a level of cohesion that just isn't possible another way.

Just as we can feel a lack of connection even when working for a pretty good company as an employee, there have been multiple times when we didn't feel like we had the right fit with a client or another group. I could often sense this intuitively, but didn't fully understand it until my experience in the final quarter of 2021.

A Textbook Example of Clearly Defined Values

I wrapped up *Leading With A Clear Purpose* by sharing how having our own extremely clear purpose helped us push through the Covid mandates that prevented us from capitalizing on the momentum we had built in our business going into 2020 and doing much billable work for anyone in the second half of that year. As some of the mandates were relaxed in early 2021, I was doing just about anything I could to create revenue and regain some of that momentum. Although I wasn't particularly excited about it, I had done quite a bit of safety and human resource consulting work for small businesses at that point.

Even while Cindy and I were still in our full-time roles, we had a few less desirable client interactions. We actually stepped away from one, which was our largest to date at the time, because of an ever-changing scope of work—after we had put in nearly half the allocated time for the entire project and the deliverables they requested continuing to change. Interestingly, some of the time spent (which was never billed to the client) became part of our *Emerging Leader Development* course—but not until a few years later. The interaction with that client, as well as some with a few smaller ones, gave us some perspective for recognizing that some juice just ain't worth the squeeze. After limping through 2020, though, I felt like I could only be so choosy.

In mid-2021, one of the small business clients I'd helped with recruiting made an email introduction between me and a couple who were acquiring a business my client had been working with for years. The couple was in the process of moving from the Gulf Coast of Florida to central Virginia. The company they were buying had been in operation for around 75 years and was about an hour away from me. Between wondering if that couple had completely lost their mind by intentionally moving from Florida's Gulf Coast—a place that Cindy and I had fallen in love with—to central Virginia, and the support they needed from me for regulations and compliance, I was reluctant to move forward. But I did, mainly because I enjoy food and sleeping inside.

My initial conversations with them were a mix of phone calls and Zoom sessions, as they hadn't yet moved to Virginia. Each of those went fine, but I still wasn't all that excited about what they needed me to help with: all the regulatory mumbo-jumbo necessary to comply with employment law when purchasing a business.

After a month or so, and at least a half dozen phone conversations, we finally had the opportunity to meet in person over dinner. Since they weren't familiar with the area and insisted on coming to us rather than having me and Cindy drive an hour to meet them, we got to choose the location. If you know us very well at all, and you're even remotely familiar with Harrisonburg, you'll understand why we opted for The Sub Station Mexican Grill!

Just in case you're not, this place has become one of our very favorites. The food is excellent, and the owners are even better. From the outside, though, especially back then, it was very easy to mistake the building for a Waffle House, since that's what it used to be. Once inside, there was little to remind you that it had previously been a hotspot for those late-night, after-the-bar crowds—other than the wooden benches in each booth, which have since been replaced.

The guy who connected us asked where we were meeting them for dinner, and was appalled. He thought I was nuts for taking a couple of their stature to what he viewed as a hole-in-the-wall. I blew him off, saying, "If they don't like me because of where we're going to eat, we probably won't get along too well on much else either!"

> **"If they don't like me because of where we're going to eat, we probably won't get along too well on much else either!"**

As it turned out, they weren't the type to turn up their noses at a place just because the waiter didn't show up at the table with a towel over his arm. We all enjoyed the interaction and the food! We were able to develop a plan for all that needed to be done as they took ownership of the business. I had quite a bit of homework to do following that conversation. However, I still didn't realize how much that interaction would help me connect the dots on just how important values are in serving as the proper foundation for any business.

A Painful Process, but with a Twist

Having been away for a few years from handling all aspects of human resources for an organization, and never dealing with an ownership transition, I left that initial dinner meeting with a list of items I needed to review before their upcoming acquisition date. Although I never liked homework, I held up my end of the bargain and was ready to roll on the morning of September 2, 2021, when the formal transition took place.

Before working through the employment verification and other forms each team member would need to complete, the long-term owners of the business introduced the entire team to Craig and Kim. While Craig and I had touched on this several times in our conversations, I genuinely enjoyed how he detailed the core values that would drive each decision they made for the company moving forward. As you can likely imagine, Craig also had to field several questions and address a few concerns at that point. In each response, I saw him exemplify each of those values: Compassion, Integrity, Humility, Family, and Dependability.

> ### In each response, I saw him exemplify each of those values: Compassion, Integrity, Humility, Family, and Dependability.

Once the paperwork was behind us, it wasn't long until we started working to fill a few positions, some to take advantage of growth opportunities and some to develop the team's bench in preparation for some pending retirements. As with any hiring I had been involved with, we needed to identify candidates with specific skills and experience. But there, more than with any other organization I had supported through a process like this, they were just as focused on any prospective team member sharing their values as they were on adequately performing the work involved. That was so refreshing, and not something I had the chance to discuss with the management team I was supporting when, just a few years prior, I hired 225 people in an eighteen-month stint.

Over the next few months, Craig and I hashed out what would be the 75+-year-old organization's first official policy manual. I had helped at least half a dozen other companies through similar processes in the decade leading up to that. While I had never enjoyed it, I had become quite effective in tying these together, juggling all the required government language while still maintaining a voice that represented the actual business. From November 2021 to mid-February 2022, we discussed every single line of the template we used as a starting point. The part of that process that stands out most was how adamant Craig and Kim were to not fill the handbook with rules for the sake of rules of rules. If we couldn't tie something directly back to one of their core values, it wasn't included in the final edition, government regulation notwithstanding, and we would have been happy to have scrapped quite a bit of that, too, given the discretion.

Once complete, our next step was to meet with the entire team in small groups to roll out the overall policy manual that, moving forward, would serve as their guide. I had done that several times as well, so I created a slide show that offered an overview of the entire thing and covered the more critical segments in detail. That went far more differently than I could have ever imagined!

A Strange but Enlightening Experience

I blocked my calendar for the afternoon of February 24, 2022, to roll out the new handbook to all team members working with Craig and Kim. Having done similar rollouts several times in the decade leading up to it, I had a clear picture in my mind of what to expect—and dreaded it. While my goal was to be brief, highlighting the specific areas everyone would want to get familiar with and touching on several of the most critical procedural guidelines, I had never seen one go quite that smoothly. Inevitably, there was that one guy in each group who was determined to pick everything apart and convince the rest of the team that management was out to get them.

As mentioned, the business was about an hour away from our office, so I left early to ensure I'd be on site well before the meetings started. In each human resource role I've held, I've always been intentional about developing relationships with every member of the organization, whether in a full-time position or a consulting role. Even then, though, I can't say that I ever received a very warm greeting before presenting what would be included in a new employee handbook. At best, I had been tolerated, and there were a few times when tolerance was nowhere to be found!

All in all, I wasn't feeling particularly optimistic about this one. Being so far away, I had only been with the team a few times, and hadn't been able to get to know the folks as well as I had leading up to other handbook rollouts. Yet from the time I walked through the door, I could tell something was different.

Our goal was to issue physical copies of the handbook, and to provide the overview as the team enjoyed a lunch provided by the owners. Since I rarely eat before presenting anything, I had a chance to mingle as everyone got their food and settled in. To prevent shutting down the retail section of the business entirely, we held three separate sessions with all team members. To a person, everyone was positive. As I wrapped up one of the sessions, one of the most senior team members—a fellow who pushed back his retirement date to help the new owners get acclimated—came to me in tears. He told me that before Craig and Kim took ownership, he had "one foot out the door and the other was on a banana peel."

He said the handbook provided him and all his coworkers with a level of clarity that he had never had before. He went on to explain that the handbook's basis of five values had been something he'd heard Craig and Kim explain routinely since the acquisition. More importantly, he had seen them live those values out in every interaction: with the team and with each customer the business served.

I won't kid you; I wasn't sure what I was experiencing. At one point, I looked around for a hidden camera! Was I being punked? Nobody thanks you for a handbook! To that end, I've never even liked those meetings. After speaking with nearly everyone that day and reflecting on it as I drove home, it was clear that their five values were not just something we had listed in the initial pages of the handbook; those values were indeed the *foundation* Craig and Kim had chosen to run and build their business.

> **It was clear that their five values were not just something we had listed in the initial pages of the handbook; those values were indeed the *foundation* Craig and Kim had chosen to run and build their business.**

While Cindy and I had various experiences with employers and other clients that highlighted the importance of values, rolling out the handbook for that organization served as a tipping point for how we wanted to run our own business, and for the ideal client we wanted to serve.

A Slight Change In Our Approach

Throughout our professional lives, Cindy and I have seen a wide range of values stated by any given organization to which we belonged. A few either had no clearly defined values to speak of, or never referenced them. Others had a couple of values listed in a policy manual or on a bulletin board, but did little to draw attention to them or explain them in more detail. A few did have thorough lists of values with explicitly written definitions for what each meant, yet did next to nothing to ensure team members exemplified those values.

In one case, I recall the organizational values being referred to as their "DNA." Folks were praised for public behaviors that aligned with those values, but no one was held accountable for actions directly opposed to them. Talk is cheap, especially when it's tied only to pomp and circumstance!

We had been delivering a keynote called "Building Buy-In Around a Clear Mission & Vision" for a few years at the time, detailing the importance of helping each team member understand how their daily behaviors tie directly to the organization's mission and vision statements. Seeing how Craig & Kim provided that same kind of clarity—for everyone in their newly acquired company—for each of their core values prompted us to begin researching how clear values provide a strong foundation for any business and produce measurable increases in overall profitability.

In addition to researching any articles we could find on the topic, we began exploring the idea with several other business owners involved in our *Executive Leadership Elite Think Tank*. We had been very intentional about only inviting folks to participate in that group who we had seen live out similar values to our own and who were focused on developing the leadership culture within their organizations. Each of them had clearly stated values in place for their companies, but what we quickly realized was that nearly all of them had opportunities for making those values a bigger part of routine conversations with their teams.

Just as our message about the difference we can make by detailing how any particular task impacts our organization's mission or vision is crucial, it's equally critical to provide specifics around the behaviors that align with or contradict our values. Even when we have a fantastic group of team members, we can't assume everyone is on the same page.

Tying Everything to Our Values

As Cindy and I worked to learn and understand what each member of our *Executive Leadership Elite Think Tank* had as core values for their organizations, we had intense conversations with all of them regarding how they kept those values in front of their teams, how often and in what setting did they cover the values, and what did applying those values look like? Like most executives, each one we talked with had far more to-do items than time to accomplish them, causing this type of intentional dialogue around core values to take a back seat to more urgent issues.

Through those conversations, however, we gained clarity on the behaviors each of them felt best demonstrated the values of their respective organizations. In many cases, we discussed scenarios involving the performance of their various team members, be they exemplary or subpar. We used such opportunities to explore how that performance aligned with or diverged from any stated value. Discussing specific situations that were fresh on their minds allowed us to help them clarify what they expected from each team member, and how they could apply each example when discussing their organization's values with their entire team.

This slight change in our approach helped those clients develop clarity around the behaviors involved in living out their values. It also provided us with a deeper understanding of how having common values with each of those executives contributed to the stronger working relationship we had built with them. More and more, we realized that the closer our values aligned with those of the individual we were working with, the better the results we achieved through that relationship. Looking back over our entire careers, we could easily see that this same thing had happened all along, whether we recognized it at the time or not.

In August 2003, John Maxwell published a book, *There's No Such Thing as "Business" Ethics*[3]. During a lesson he offered around that time, he shared how he'd initially turned down his publisher when they asked him to write something on "Business Ethics." When they pressed him on why he wouldn't write on the topic, he said, "There's no such thing as 'business ethics'; there's just *ethics*. You either have them, or you don't."

I'll come back to ethics soon. For now, I'll share that I believe one of the most important things we can do with our values in our professional or personal lives is to make sure we have a clear understanding of the exact behavior necessary to uphold them. When we have this in place and can keep it top of mind in our own routine, we have a much better chance of providing the same clarity for the team members who count on us for leadership. Then, we'll only need to make slight adjustments to our daily routines to keep those values front and center. I'll share a simple example of how Cindy and I have worked to achieve this now. Later on, we'll work through some specific steps that any leader can take to make this part of their daily routine.

Changes We Had to Make

As we developed more clarity around the values of the clients we enjoyed working with the most, we found more and more opportunities to challenge them on how to tie those values to nearly every conversation they had with their teams. This didn't require significant changes in what they were already doing; it just needed a touch of intentionality in the message they shared. With each of those clients, it was fairly routine to discuss their team members' performance, specifically how that performance contributed to the overall productivity and profitability of their organizations. The slight change we made in those conversations was to press each executive on how they could connect the employee's behavior, which contributed to or detracted from productivity and profitability, to any of their stated core values. While this initially required some prodding, mainly because it hadn't been something they had ever considered in depth before, it quickly became second nature—at least when we specifically asked them about it.

Making the connection, when pressed, during a one-on-one conversation, and communicating those connections with the team member in a real-life scenario, proved to be two very different things. One of the first things I learned during my initial training on behavior-based safety was the power of habit. Depending on the source, it generally takes 21 to 30 days to develop a new habit or change an existing one, assuming we can perform the behavior tied to the desired habit routinely without slipping back into our previous behavior. Whether that's biting our fingernails, smoking cigarettes, or intentionally connecting a team member's behavior to our values, making a change once doesn't equate to sustaining that change. Through our conversations with those clients, we realized we needed to be just as intentional about helping them maintain their slight changes as we were in working with them to make the connections in the first place. Since then, we've rarely had a conversation with any client, existing or prospective, without discussing their values.

While we were developing a clear understanding of how to best support our client—in keeping their values visible throughout their teams—I must admit that we did not have the same clarity around our own values. After more than two decades of marriage and involvement in several business projects together, even before launching Dove Development & Consulting, Cindy and I had a strong sense of what we valued most. That said, we'd only discussed those in general terms for ourselves and concerning the words or phrases any particular client listed as their values. Unfortunately, even with what I felt were some deeply held personal values in mind, I hadn't taken the time to specify them, or detail the behaviors required to practice them daily.

We'll look more at the specifics of this later. For now, know the significance of simply putting one's values to paper and outlining what someone should see us doing to model them. Doing this also helped us be even more effective in supporting our clients as they worked through the same process. Before we begin working through any of those steps in detail, consider this quick example of how we've seen closely held and consistently communicated values directly impact a business's bottom line.

Living, Breathing Proof

Over the course of my close to fifty years on this ball of mud, I've learned that the only people who genuinely like change are the ones who came up with the idea for the specific change that's happening at any given moment. I can tolerate change when I have some level of control over how it occurs, or when I can see how that change can immediately yield better results.

All in all, though, I still believe I adapt to change better than most people. Yet I'm not willing to blindly accept random changes just for the sake of saying we've made a change. Having so many experiences prove how values indeed provide a strong foundation for any business—and specifically the textbook example leading up to the handbook rollout—it was not too difficult to absorb the changes we made to our prior personal and business values.

Telling you that values are important is easy, though. For years, I worked with a supervisor who coined the phrase, "A mouth will say anything," which he would usually insert into a conversation after one of his employees made a nonsensical excuse for why they had done something they shouldn't have. Since he's retired, he seems to reserve that more for political candidates! With that in mind, I'll share the results that rapidly followed the textbook example I detailed earlier.

By the end of their second year of ownership, the business Craig and Kim led had increased overall revenue by fifty percent. During that process, they may have experienced five percent voluntary turnover over the entire twenty-four-month span. For perspective, the Bureau of Labor Statistics[4] estimates the average annual voluntary turnover rate at just under 25%; they had less than one-fifth of that in twice the time! Additionally, they were able to provide significant wage increases for every role and institute some new incentive plans. Since the two-year mark, they've purchased three additional businesses, each complementing the existing business and providing collaborative opportunities across the entire organization.

I won't pretend they haven't experienced bumps along the way. Nothing goes that smoothly. But through every step of the process, I've watched Craig and Kim keep their core values at the forefront. Each decision they make in handling a demanding customer ties back to their values. Interactions with every employee, every single day, are based on those values. At this point, the reputation they're building in the community demonstrates how much those values truly matter.

> **Each decision they make in handling a demanding customer ties back to their values. Interactions with every employee, every single day, are based on those values. At this point, the reputation they're building in the community demonstrates how much those values truly matter.**

Make no mistake, though: none of the growth they've achieved has fallen into their laps. Listing the values in their handbook and printing them on the back of their shirts, would have made little impact had they not **followed through** in their daily routine. The challenge in far too many businesses today is that even the most articulate values rarely get attention after the ink is dry. Before we work through specific steps to ensure a business is built on values, let's examine how even the best values on paper may not be effective if they're not being practiced...

CHAPTER TWO

WHAT HAPPENS WHEN FOUNDATIONAL VALUES AREN'T IN PLACE?

What Can a Lack of Values Cost Us?

The interaction we've had with Craig, Kim, and their team over the years since they acquired their business, has provided us with a great deal of clarity on the critical role values can play in a company. This experience has also helped us develop a clearer picture of who we can best serve through the work we're doing. If we don't align with a client on values, the juice won't likely be worth the squeeze for us or them. The biggest challenge, though, has been determining where the rubber really meets the road regarding a stated set of values in any organization.

Having just shared the growth Craig and Kim's business (much of which ties directly to their emphasis on a clear set of values), we'll look at some examples of what can happen when values aren't modeled soon.

Before doing so, I was hoping to offer some hard, statistically proven data to show precisely what companies with clearly defined values yield in terms of profitability increases. Unfortunately, that data is tough to locate—if it exists at all! For now, I'll share how Curt Steinhorst closed his Forbes.com article called "Rethinking the Value of Core Values[5]":

> "Core values have weight, especially when they're *truthful* and *focused on what matters to the community* within the organization. If they're hollow, corrupted, misguided, or pretentious, they carry with them a falsehood that can trap and divide an organization. But if they are drawn from and

representative of the community they serve, they can have the strength of steel. Like any principle or strategy, core values are difficult to forge and take time to develop and cure, but once they're well-formed, they sustain you through everything else."

If my eyes weren't playing tricks on me, and that 50% increase in revenue that Craig and Kim experienced in just twenty-four months of owning their business really did have something to do with their closely held values, why couldn't I find a mountain of data with detailed examples backing Steinhorst's statement? I certainly agree with it!

It may tie back to what Pat Lencioni shared in a Harvard Business Review article called "Make Your Values Mean Something[6]" more than two decades ago:

> "Given all the hard work that goes into developing and implementing a solid values system, most companies would probably prefer not to bother. And indeed they shouldn't, because poorly implemented values can poison a company's culture."

Maybe, just maybe, the work I saw Craig and Kim do to embed a clear set of values into the culture of their new company isn't something many other business owners or executives are willing to do. But why is that? Most of the studies I read as I attempted to find that hard data showed that around 80% of companies today have their core values detailed on their website.

Let's examine the likely source of the disconnect.

How Clear Is Clear Enough?

In my experience over the last two decades, I can't point to a single company that I've worked for or with where no values were listed anywhere, whether in the employee handbook or painted prominently on walls throughout the facility. Much of my experience with those organizations involved taking new employees through the orientation process, so I was exposed quite a bit to those values. Not only was I covering the high points of the policy manual, those sessions were typically held in a room with the values listed somewhere within sight. And if not directly inside the room, they were definitely on a bulletin board just outside.

Even if we never worked together or for the same companies, I have no doubt you can picture yourself in a setting like this as a new employee—or at least in a meeting room where you can see the values listed. But how often did you hear anyone discuss those values after that initial orientation? And where else did you see the values referenced?

In an article from MIT Sloan Management Review called "When It Comes to Culture, Does Your Company Walk the Talk?[7]", the authors open with this:

> "When Johnson & Johnson's CEO codified the company's principles into a credo in 1943, corporate value statements were a novelty. Today they are ubiquitous among large corporations. In our study of nearly 700 large companies, we found that more than 80% published an official set of corporate values on their website. Senior leaders, in particular, love to talk about their company culture. Over the past three decades, more than three-quarters of CEOs interviewed in a major business magazine discussed their company's culture or core values — even when not specifically asked about it. Corporate values statements are nearly universal, but do they matter? Critics dismiss them as cheap talk with no impact on employees' day-to-day behavior."

While I found more statistics on the frequency of visible company core values, I could find no direct correlation between this and its impact on revenue, as opposed to the remaining minority without clearly stated values. To get a clear picture of what that lack of core values costs, I believe our best bet would be to circle back to *What's KILLING Your Profitability?*, because there's sure to be a gap in leadership if we're not at least upholding a set of core values.

For now, let's consider how so many companies could have their values listed on a website, in a handbook, and posted throughout their buildings, with there still being room for critics to dismiss them. And suppose CEOs are speaking about their values so frequently, even without being asked to do so. In that case, there should be substantial evidence showing the impact it has on their organizations' bottom line! Shouldn't that make any organizational values clear enough for everyone involved?

Several factors are driving this disconnect, providing critics (and often the employees in those companies) with more than enough reason to blow the stated values off as cheap talk. Think about the latter first: how frequently is the CEO from one of those "large corporations" referenced in that study likely to interact with the minions? I mean, their employees… It's one thing to pontificate for the media and Wall Street, but do you really think they're singing the same song on the rare occasion they talk with someone on the front line?

Now, the former… At least those values are listed in plenty of places so that every employee can read them, and all other levels of management can carry the torch, right? How often have you heard values discussed openly after the first day with a company (or the day an updated handbook is rolled out)? And where were the managers or supervisors in that process? If they were even in the room, I'd guess they weren't the ones talking! Oh, and how much clarity were you given for what anything in that word salad actually meant, or looked like in practice?

The authors of the MIT Sloan article went on to say, "Unfortunately, many organizations' core values are so generic that they could easily serve as fodder for a *Dilbert* cartoon." What a far too-relevant statement.

Values Pushed to the Back Burner?

Before we dig into the challenges that come with "core values so generic that they could easily serve as fodder for a *Dilbert* cartoon," we need to think about how that could ever be the case when "more than three-quarters of CEOs interviewed in a major business magazine discussed their company's culture of core values—even when not specifically asked about it." If it sounded like I was taking a shot at those CEOs for jumping on their soapbox for the media but not investing the time to share an articulate message with everyone in their organizations, it's because I was! But I am willing to concede that not all of them make a conscious decision to shun their team members while puffing their chests for the camera.

The reality is, accepting any leadership role means abolishing whatever spare time we might've had in our previous role. There's never a shortage of issues demanding our attention; some are urgent because a ball was dropped, and others are less urgent but still absolutely critical within our scope of responsibility. With that in mind, I have no doubt that the CEOs of the large companies referenced in the MIT Sloan article interact with journalists, investors, and their board members far more frequently than they're able to speak face-to-face with the majority of the people on their teams. I'll go out on a limb here and bet that much personal interaction beyond their executive team members just doesn't routinely fit into their schedules.

Most of that is likely focused on whatever fire needs to be doused on that particular day. I'd go so far as to guess that, even then, those core values that get attention (whether they're asked about them or not) are placed on the back burner at that point—if they're still on the stovetop at all!

Truthfully, if that were you or me, wouldn't we expect our executive team to be in lockstep with us on the values we've spoken about publicly and have printed on the walls and in our handbook? We certainly don't have time to rehash those daily, especially not with the folks we're counting on to lead their respective teams! Do we?

You likely sense sarcasm here, and you should. While I'm convinced that this is what goes through the mind of many a CEO, whether they're heading up one of the large companies referenced in the article or running their own small business, this is all too often when even the simplest, most clearly stated values can begin to unravel. When we get consumed by the work that has to be addressed at the moment, allowing the urgent to take precedence over the important, or even worse, we assume everyone paid attention the one time we did talk about our values, we leave room for the even the best of our folks who may have actually paid attention initially (or even read the handbook) to form their own definition for what each core value looks like in practice. That may be OK in the short term, but it can result in devastating consequences as, over time, those definitions drift.

> **We get consumed by the work that has to be addressed at the moment, allowing the urgent to take precedence over the important.**

Without Living Our Values, Things Can Go REALLY Wrong!

In early December of 2001, I was just getting my feet under me in the behavior-based safety role I had accepted in the spring of that year, doing all I could to take care of our young family and still reeling a bit from our freedom being attacked just a few months prior. I recall seeing the headlines detailing Enron's filing for bankruptcy, but I won't pretend I had a finger on the pulse of all it meant or how it unfolded. In the months and years that followed, however, I read plenty about what a lack of values ultimately cost many people who had ties to that organization.

Since that happened more than two decades ago, and since even a shit show that big was overshadowed by what ended up becoming a global war on terror, let's take a walk down memory lane. There's no shortage of summary articles, but here's one I found called "Enron Code of Ethics[8]" on fbi.gov, a source I would have considered very reliable just a few years ago: "The executives of Enron defrauded thousands of people out of their life savings, leading to financial ruin for many of the employees that they purported to hold to high ethical standards."

The article provides a comprehensive snapshot of what unfolded and a wide-shot of the investigation(s) that followed. After explaining just how much data was seized as evidence, retired Supervisory Special Agent Michael E. Anderson, who led the Enron Task Force in Houston, was quoted as sharing this:

"Enron was a company where it was OK to lie; it was OK to cheat as long as you were making money for the company. And that attitude was permissible up to the top levels of the company. Both Skilling and Lay [the former CEOs of Enron], they agreed with that, and they allowed employees, they tolerated transgressions as long as employees were making money for the company."

> **It was OK to cheat as long as you were making money for the company. And that attitude was permissible up to the top levels of the company.**

As we began this journey, I shared my recent experience working with a company that provided a textbook example of how clearly defined values can positively impact each team member and drive substantial increases in revenue and profitability. If we were to take a quick look at the two side by side, we could easily assume that Enron lacked clear values—and we'd be wrong! While there was clearly a lack of living out their values, they did have a clear set posted for the world to see.

Strong Values & Clear Definitions that Fell Flat

As an organization, Enron had indeed identified its values:

Respect: We treat others as we would like to be treated ourselves. We do not tolerate abusive or disrespectful treatment. Ruthlessness, callousness and arrogance don't belong here.

Integrity: We work with customers and prospects openly, honestly and sincerely. When we say we will do something, we will do it; when we say we cannot or will not do something, then we won't do it.

Communication: We have an obligation to communicate. Here, we take the time to talk with one another...and to listen. We believe that information is meant to move and that information moves people.

Excellence: We are satisfied with nothing less than the very best in everything we do. We will continue to raise the bar for everyone. The great fun here will be for all of us to discover just how good we can really be.

I pulled this list from Enron's "Statement of Human Rights Principles[9]," as shared on the Sacramento State University website.

Now, think back to the statement made by Supervisory Special Agent Michael E. Anderson: "Enron was a company where it was OK to lie; it was OK to cheat as long as you were making money for the company."

Cindy and I initially shared a lesson with our *Executive Leadership Elite Think Tank*, then developed that lesson into a half-day workshop for several of the organizations represented in that group, where we emphasized the values of respect, integrity, communication, and excellence. We challenged the individuals in each group to describe what came to mind when they heard those words.

While definitions varied some, they weren't far off from what you see from Enron above. Quite frankly, those are some of the clearest and best-stated values I've seen. Somewhere along the line, though, that train ran off the tracks! When we shared the name of the organization from which those values came, nearly everyone's chin dropped.

Unfortunately, it's not uncommon for even the strongest values, with the most precise definitions, to be detailed in a handbook and painted on the walls of the organization while even some of the most senior supervisors and managers struggle to list them.

> **It's not uncommon for even the strongest values, with the most precise definitions, to be detailed in a handbook and painted on the walls of the organization while even some of the most senior supervisors and managers struggle to list them.**

Recently, we opened a session with a group by asking for volunteers to share their values. While a few offered ideas off the top of their head, no one could list any of the company's actual core values—and those values were painted on the wall in the room...

Make no mistake: I'm not placing blame on anyone in that group. All too often, we're caught up in the urgency of the day-to-day and lose sight of the clear purpose that should be driving us and the values that define who we are as an organization. While our team may be mostly dialed in, we cannot afford to let the definitions of those values drift. And they absolutely will if we're not constantly discussing them in detail, so we'll work through that soon. First, though, we need to understand just how easy it can be for any one of us to drift, ever so slightly, away from even the most clearly defined values.

No One Chooses to Fall Flat

I can point to dozens of powerful lessons I learned in the decade and a half I had direct involvement in behavior-based safety. While the initiative focused on identifying and mitigating risks to the workforce, it provided a hands-on look at why people behave the way they do. I'd put that real-world experience up against any kind of degree in psychology all day long!

While it's not the lesson I reference most often, recognizing that no one gets out of bed on any given day hoping to have an accident certainly ranks in the top ten. I'm guessing you just rolled your eyes (at least a little bit). Duh, Wes, of course no one would do that. Yet, every single day, we all do things that put us at risk of injury— sometimes death! My initial training in the behavior-based safety concept in 1998 taught me not only how to recognize the actions someone takes that can expose them to injury, but also how to ask open-ended questions to identify why they chose (yes, *chose*) to do something that could get them hurt.

> **No one gets out of bed on any given day hoping to have an accident. Yet, every single day, we all do things that put us at risk of injury**

The responses ranged from "I didn't realize I was so close to being injured," to "That's the only way the job can be done," to "I have to do it that way to make my numbers." As you likely imagine, we received many other replies as well; those were just some of the most common. In each case, though, the reason for choosing the behavior did nothing to prevent an injury. To compound that, the risks to which someone was exposed typically became more significant—performing risky actions with no consequences only further reinforced that behavior as an acceptable approach to the job. And with that reinforcement came more confidence for assuming even higher levels of risk. Unfortunately, the worst workplace injuries I ever dealt with were ones where someone had taken (often multiple) risks in doing their job for years without the slightest issue.

During my time in human resources, where I dealt with some of the most challenging scenarios imaginable in the workplace, I often had to reflect on this. Just as no one wakes up hoping to get hurt at some point in their day, people rarely *want* to do a poor job or be perceived as a bad person. Without revisiting that thought, having multiple disciplinary action conversations each day would leave me with a worldview that was more than a little jaded.

With that in mind, let's consider how strong values with clear definitions could fall flat. If Enron employees were exposed to the detailed values I shared before, even occasionally, I can't picture many folks consciously choosing to violate them. The words alone, without the concise definitions detailing what each meant for the organization, provided most of them with a firm reference for how they should conduct business. But, like taking incrementally more risks for being injured, I can understand how the pressures to achieve organizational targets could lead to pushing the boundaries of any one of those values; a little at first, but more and more over time as the results met those targets without the behavior that produced those results being called into question. I'd guess situations where someone wildly violated any specific value were few and far between. However, even the slightest ambiguity surrounding exactly how the value applied to a particular scenario allowed the individual involved to form their own definition, which justified why it was necessary and only slightly pushed the boundary those values provided.

When results get more attention than the behaviors that led to those results, you can bet those behaviors will get repeated! In far too many cases, business owners and high-level executives are caught up in the urgency of the daily tasks and drift away from ensuring that the message they share with their teams, the managers they rely on to run their businesses, includes clear definitions for their organizational values. And that opens the door to the slippery slope that leads to a fall!

Why Do So Many Miss the Mark on Values?

I've never seen an organization's executive team intentionally neglect living out its values, especially if they had a clear understanding of how much doing so could cost them. Whether it's intentional or not, it happens more often than any of us likely realize. But how can that be when companies have established routines for communicating their core values?

During the last two years that I worked in a large manufacturing facility, I led the new hire orientation process for more than three hundred people. At that point, my responsibility was to issue policy manuals and cover the most critical details that, from then on, they'd be expected to understand. In addition to attendance expectations and work rules, I covered the company's mission statement, which also served as the corporate quality policy. (That was also printed on the back of the ID badge they'd be using to clock in and out each day).

Even after being drastically condensed by whoever handled such matters from an office just north of Chicago, the mission statement was still quite wordy. I knew no one would actually memorize it—I certainly hadn't in the more than fifteen years I had worked for the company leading up to that point—so I focused on the key points I felt were most critical to what those new employees would encounter in their roles daily. While this was the closest thing I can recall to covering the company's core values during those orientation sessions, I'm unsure if what I explained actually aligned with what you would have found on the organization's website. To that end, I'm not sure I ever knew the core values listed on the website.

The rest of that half-day orientation included some basics from the safety manager and quality manager. The final half of their first day would be spent in the departments to which they'd be assigned moving forward, albeit not always at the same equipment, or even on the same shift. From the moment those new team members arrived on the manufacturing floor, they were inundated with how-to guides specifically tailored to their new positions. I'll let you guess how often any of that ever tied back to the company's core values.

In the decade leading up to my full-time role in human resources, I held a different position in the new hire orientation process. I shared a brief overview of the behavior-based safety concept during the initial half-day session, then provided four full hours of training on hazard recognition at the end of their first week. Since the new team members had been exposed to at least some of what they'd be doing in their regular roles by that time, I could go into quite a bit of detail about how they could ensure their behavior was in line with our safety rules. With any luck, that would serve as a foundation for helping them go home each day with all the parts they had when they came in.

Similarly, their on-the-job training provided a step-by-step approach to operating the assigned piece of equipment. An experienced operator would guide them through performing each task, or setting up the equipment to produce a quality product without damaging any tooling, all while hopefully avoiding injury. Similar to what I was attempting to provide through the behavior-based safety and hazard recognition training, the individuals training these new employees provided visual examples of the work they'd be expected to perform.

While safety, quality, and productivity were critical to the organization's success, I can't honestly tell you that they were listed specifically as core values. And if I couldn't list or define the core values, as one of less than forty salaried employees in the facility during my final two years with the organization, what are the odds of any one of those 300 new employees—or any of the other employees for that matter—knowing exactly what those values were, let alone how they could live them out in their daily routine? We may have occasionally touched on the values listed in the handbook, but I assure you it wasn't enough to sink in.

Make no mistake: I don't share this to shame that organization. Quite honestly, the emphasis we placed on safety, quality, and productivity has been something I've been able to model in helping many other companies since. I'm just sharing that values didn't receive a lot of specific attention, and I'll bet you've had similar experiences.

With that in mind, let's examine how straightforward it is to make a change.

What Message Are We Consistently Sharing?

To understand why many organizations fail to provide a clear and consistent representation of the values outlined in their policy manuals or on their websites, we need to consider what we are emphasizing clearly and consistently with our teams. During the nearly two decades I spent working for a global leader in the automotive parts manufacturing sector, the topics I heard about most frequently were safety, quality, stock price, and productivity—but in that exact opposite order. As I mentioned before, our mission statement contained numerous buzzwords, many of which can be found in quite a few other company's mission statements. Still, I can't say with certainty whether any of those were our actual corporate values.

However, I can recall with remarkable clarity how often productivity was discussed: *DAILY* at nearly every level within our local facility, which tells me it was just as hot a topic at every other level up the food chain. When I operated a press, I knew exactly how many parts I was expected to churn out each day. Everyone in each manufacturing area had direct visibility of productivity for the previous day, week, month, and quarter—assuming they paid any attention whatsoever.

I also remember how frequently we heard about the company's stock price, as well as the hoops we'd need to jump through for the final ten weeks of each quarter (yes, you read that right) to ensure the earnings statement met Wall Street's expectations. Safety and quality were frequent conversation points as well; they were just more casual until we received a significant complaint from a customer, or a serious injury occurred.

While each of those things is imperative to an organization's success, I still can't tell you how they tied back to whatever had been defined as our core values. Having shared my poor recollection of those values a few times now, I can see where I might be giving you the impression I wasn't fully engaged. Truth be told, I believe I was as dialed in on that company achieving outstanding results as anyone in our local facility; I knew every employee on a first-name basis, and I had friends and family who had worked there since it opened in the early 60s, not to mention it being how I kept the lights on for my family!

Regarding productivity, safety, and quality, we all had a clear understanding of what we were expected to do daily. In many cases, specifically through our behavior-based safety initiative, individuals knew exactly what behaviors were necessary for avoiding risks, because they received feedback and guidance on their individual roles. For each of those metrics, there was little room left for individual discretion as to what was acceptable and what was not. I think you know the answer to how all that relates to that company's values, so I'll ask if you have the same level of understanding about your organization's values.

Defining Exactly How It's Done

In March, April, and May 1996, I received extensive one-on-one training on how to operate the various pieces of equipment to which I was assigned. Initially, someone else was responsible for swapping out the tooling and dies after each order I completed so the next part could be made. For a while, at least until I got proficient in the repetitive movements required to run those presses, the guy doing those setups would have another machine ready for me before I finished.

Once I found my rhythm, he could no longer stay ahead of me, and that allowed me to start looking over his shoulder and ask questions. I didn't feel all that mechanically inclined, but I also didn't enjoy standing around or waiting on someone else so I could get started on my next job. Thus, I was chomping at the bit to learn how to do those setups myself. Just like learning to operate each piece of equipment, the person training me to do those setups and change-overs walked me through every step of the process. They showed me exactly what needed to be done, what adjustments I'd need to make, and what to watch out for through it all. Whether it was running the machine to stamp out parts or making the changes necessary to produce the next order, understanding each specific behavior necessary played a key role in being efficient, but it also had a direct impact on the quality of those parts, and it helped me avoid getting hurt—and in a manufacturing facility, significant injuries can happen in a split second!

> **They showed me exactly what needed to be done, what adjustments I'd need to make, and what to watch out for through it all.**

Over the next several years, I became proficient in running, setting up and troubleshooting most of the equipment in my home department. During that time, I trained several new individuals using the same approach that had been used with me. As I transitioned to behavior-based safety, I learned how to be just as specific when discussing with my peers how the actions they took while performing their jobs either helped them avoid, or exposed them, to the potential for workplace injuries. The common thread was being specific about how their behaviors impacted their results. Had any of those interactions provided only vague generalities, I doubt many of those individuals would have gained a fundamental understanding, leaving them to fill in the gaps on their own.

Over the last year or so, a nearby town has had its share of drama. I won't bother sharing even what I know, which is limited to what's spilled out of the rumor mill. From what I can tell, though, only a select few know the behind-the-scenes details. However, that certainly hasn't stopped people on every side of each issue from creating their own narrative about who is corrupt or what the next conspiracy theory is. Without a transparent explanation for each of the scenarios that have got the folks in and around that town all riled up, they've been left to fill in the gaps—mostly on social media. While it does offer a bit of entertainment value, it's far from productive (or positive) for anyone involved.

Had the training I was receiving on those machines lacked detail of any kind, I would have had to fill in the gaps myself—just the folks around that town as they heard random rumors. Unfortunately, failing to share a consistent message about exactly what it looks like to apply our values can result in the same thing. Even when we have our values printed in handbooks and on the wall, we run the risk of ambiguity—and that can set the stage for things to go downhill quickly. Preventing this is simple, though, so we'll dig into that next!

CHAPTER THREE

WHAT DO YOUR VALUES REALLY MEAN?

How many times have you provided one of your team members with directions for completing a task you needed their help with to get wrapped up by a particular time only to end up with something far different from what you had hoped? I'm sure we've all been on both ends of scenarios like that. We knew exactly what we meant when we asked for help, but somehow, it got lost in translation.

Think back to the four specific values I shared previously—*respect, integrity, communication, and excellence*—and consider how much variance could creep in, even with such simple wording and relatively clear definitions included, if every individual involved had to decide for themselves exactly how they were to apply those in their respective roles. Then, add all the other daily stresses of a to-do list, plus a fair amount of pressure to drive revenue in a way that makes a stockholder happy. I have vivid memories of watching the games that were played to make the quarterly numbers look good for Wall Street, and the company I worked for never came close to having a mess the size of Enron's. With even the slightest ambiguity around our values, even the most elaborate definitions won't do much to prevent things from going wrong—especially when the most significant rewards are going to those who openly skirt the boundaries of those values.

Clear Words, Ambiguous Understanding

To understand why so many organizations miss the mark in exemplifying their core business values or even making sure everyone on the team knows what they are, take a look at how an article called "The Impact of Organizational Ambiguity on Performance Evaluation Metrics[10]" opened:

Organizational ambiguity, often defined as the presence of uncertainty in decision-making processes, plays a significant role in shaping business dynamics. In a recent study by McKinsey & Company, it was revealed that over 70% of executives reported experiencing high levels of ambiguity during strategic planning. This phenomenon can affect everything from employee morale to overall productivity, with companies facing up to a 25% drop in performance when key stakeholders are uncertain about the direction of their initiatives. The story of a leading tech firm illustrates this point vividly; as they expanded globally, inconsistent messaging led to confusion among teams, resulting in a staggering $75 million loss attributed to misaligned goals and unclear expectations.

> **Inconsistent messaging led to confusion among teams, resulting in a staggering $75 million loss attributed to misaligned goals and unclear expectations.**

The concept of organizational ambiguity is not merely an abstract idea; it manifests itself in very tangible ways within organizations. According to a study published in the Harvard Business Review, organizations with high levels of clarity in communication saw a 32% improvement in employee engagement scores compared to those who struggled with ambiguity.

The organization that published this was explicitly focused on the importance of providing clear feedback during performance evaluations (and how their product or service aided with that), and we'll touch on that more soon. For now, let's consider how unlikely it would be for individuals in the organizations they studied to have much clarity when more than 70% of the executives admitted to "high levels of ambiguity." John Maxwell's famous quote, "Everything rises and falls on leadership," immediately comes to my mind!

What do you think the chances are that, if you and I were operating under those four relatively simple values but felt tremendous pressure to achieve results (especially if we were aware of a "25% drop in performance" stemming from "uncertainty about the direction" of our organization's initiatives) we'd have different ideas for how those values applied to our work? Even if your picture only varied slightly from mine, the difference in how we approached our work could be dramatic—and that's assuming both of us knew the core values of the business. That's nowhere near a safe assumption we should make.

Sometimes Ambiguous, Sometimes Completely Unknown

Each time we kick off our *Emerging Leader Development* course, Cindy and I open with a slide detailing the importance of having and exemplifying core business values. In one of the first we ever provided on-site for a large organization, Cindy shared her experience serving on the Maxwell Leadership President's Advisory Council, learning not just the acronym for remembering their values but what each of those values looked like for members of that group. I followed that by sharing some of the general ideas that most companies have at least woven into their values—such as safety, quality, or service—then asked that very seasoned group of supervisors and managers to list their organizational values.

A few of them fumbled through random guesses before one of them could no longer stand the awkwardness and blurted out that no one in the room had any idea what their corporate office listed as their formal values. As awkward as that moment was, his blunt comment brought an end to the suffering. Feeling like I had reopened an old wound, I changed gears and challenged the group to develop a list of values they could rally their respective teams around, with the hope of not drawing too much undesired attention to how any existing values within the company had (or had not) been communicated. Since that time, we've been very intentional in asking about the organization's specific values before starting a training session.

As uncomfortable as I was when that happened, I shouldn't have been surprised. As I mentioned earlier, I can't list the stated values of the organization I spent nearly two decades with, during which I was involved in the new hire onboarding process for three-quarters of that time. Even with a well-intended initiative to roll out values from the ivory tower (corporate office), George Bernard Shaw's statement can ring far too true; "The single biggest problem in communication is the illusion that it has taken place."[11]

> **"The single biggest problem in communication is the illusion that it has taken place."**

Even in a few of the cases where we discussed the organization's values in detail with the manager or owner bringing us on-site, we've still seen a lot of folks with the deer-in-the-headlights look when we've asked them to detail their company's values; think back to the example I shared where those values were on the wall in the room and the participants still struggled to list them.

With each of these situations fresh in mind, should we really be surprised with how things unfolded at Enron, even with values as simple as *respect, integrity, communication, and excellence*? While each had basic and clear definitions listed to provide more context, I can certainly understand how other, more immediate pressures could cause employees to bend each to fit what they felt they had to do to hit their targets.

Before we delve into how infrequently people understand the behavior required to meet expectations or what we can do to address this issue, let's consider what ambiguity is costing our organizations. I realize that the article I referenced earlier, which detailed a large tech firm's "staggering $75 million loss attributed to misaligned goals and unclear expectations," may not resonate with most of us, as most of us aren't working in large tech firms. Without knowing the name of that firm, who knows what percentage of their revenue or profit that represents? While we could write it off that easily, could you come up with a better way of using that $75 million, regardless of the percentage? Since I know that answer, let's look at how we can connect those statistics to our own situation.

Ambiguity Carries a High Cost

Since the large tech firm's "staggering $75 million loss attributed to misaligned goals and unclear expectations," which I've referenced twice now, could be more than you or I will experience in our own roles, let's make it a bit more personal and consider what our numbers could be... First, though, let's examine the issue from a global perspective—to eliminate any possibility of thinking this could never apply to us. Here's how an article I found called "Why Ambiguity Leads to Lower Work Performance[12]" opened:

> Fear of the unknown is a natural emotion that is part of being human. However, when ambiguity arises in the work context, its effects can be detrimental to performance.
>
> According to recent research, "Uncertainty about a possible future threat disrupts our ability to avoid it or to mitigate its negative impact, and thus results in anxiety." Unfortunately, anxiety is a very common problem, affecting most, if not all of us, from time to time.
>
> Taking steps to reduce anxiety in the workplace is not just a nice gesture but one that protects an organization's bottom line. According to the World Health Organization, anxiety can have a detrimental effect, costing nearly $1 trillion in lost productivity worldwide.

> **According to the World Health Organization, anxiety can have a detrimental effect, costing nearly $1 trillion in lost productivity worldwide.**

My primary goal in writing *Leading With A Clear Purpose* was to emphasize the importance of having a definite understanding of exactly *why* we do what we do each day, both as leaders throughout our entire organizations and as individual contributors on a team. That clear purpose should provide us with a big-picture view to work toward, but our values serve as the foundation for *how* we go about achieving that purpose on any given day. When there's ambiguity around that *how*, we shouldn't be surprised to learn that "anxiety is a very common problem" for the team members counting on us for clarity.

Now, let's consider the specific impact this has on our organizations when we leave room for ambiguity, particularly regarding the values that should guide our team's behavior. The same article that detailed the $75 million loss—and that 70% of the executives they surveyed admitted to ambiguity in their strategic plans—also shared that, "This phenomenon can affect everything from employee morale to overall productivity, with companies facing up to a 25% drop in performance when key stakeholders are uncertain about the direction of their initiatives."

Many of the smaller businesses that Cindy and I work with operate primarily on a billable-hour basis. For the first six or seven years of our business, that's what kept our lights on, too. In many of the other companies we support, contracts are based on completing large projects or providing a set amount of a specific product for a predetermined amount. Regardless of how the terms are negotiated or how payment is made, some form of labor is involved in each.

Let's put ourselves in an imaginary world where the work all our team members do during the forty hours they're on the job each week is directly tied to what our customer pays for. How would our organization's output change if those billable hours (or whatever they're called in your specific situation) dropped by 25%, leaving you with just 30 hours contributing to what your customers are paying for? We'd certainly see a significant dip in the amount of anything we're delivering, but we'd also see a massive hit in profit margin— because we're still paying them for all forty hours, and all of our other fixed costs are the same.

I realize this analogy leaves you filling in many of the blanks, but I hope it conveys just how quickly ambiguity can impact the bottom line of any business. We all hope for top-level performance from our teams. Far too often, though, even the slightest bit of ambiguity can leave those team members wondering what that top-level performance looks like and what they need to do to achieve it. Our responsibility as leaders lies in removing that ambiguity and providing clear expectations.

Removing the Ambiguity

If we want to have any chance of removing the ambiguity that too frequently surrounds the values listed on our conference room walls and detailed in the first few pages of our employee handbooks, we'd better share specific examples of what those core values look like in the workplace. To ensure our team members understand exactly what those values mean and how each relates to their daily work, it's up to us (as leaders) to share examples of how our company values are put into action.

> ## It's up to us (as leaders) to share examples of how our company values are put into action.

Early in our *Emerging Leader Development* course, and as often as I can find a reason to do so, I share what John Maxwell told me and a couple hundred other people during a small session in Orlando just before a larger event to certify a few thousand people from around the world to use his material. John emphasized that once we completed the licensing process to train on the content he had poured his life into, he expected each of us always to exceed the expectations of every client we worked with. He went on to share these numbers: "80% of people fall short of what's expected, around 15% do just what's expected, and only 5% will ever put in the extra work to exceed expectations."

The point I make after repeating John's statistics is that we won't have much competition when we're willing to do the work necessary to consistently be part of the 5% who exceed expectations. I'm convinced the percentage we're competing with has decreased significantly since he shared that with us in August 2015!

Never one to set an expectation without providing a clear explanation of how we could achieve it, John went on to teach those of us in that small group a short but powerful lesson on how he works with each organization he serves to be sure he understands precisely what they expect from him and how he identifies ways he can deliver more than they expect. While the first step was simply asking the client to share their expectations, he went on to detail the specific questions he asked to gauge their response, thereby developing a clear picture of what results they hoped to achieve afterward. Understanding their goals and learning key information about their organization allows him to tailor his message to be more applicable to everyone in the audience. If you've seen John speak with various groups, using similar stories or points to connect in different ways, you can bet those tweaks were based on what he learned from his host in advance when he asked what they expected from him.

Over the last decade, that quick lesson has served me and Cindy extremely well. Without having a specific understanding of what someone expects us to deliver (in writing), we've found that it's rarely worth providing so much as a ballpark price structure. Even if there's an initial agreement on price, it's incredibly hard to hit a target that has yet to be identified. While this can be abstract in what we do, it's certainly not the case in most businesses. Think about it: would you ever ask a contractor to price a building without providing the size, location, and at least a rough idea of the materials involved?

With all that in mind, let's think about what most organizations do when sharing their core values. How much detail do we provide for the folks we're onboarding to ensure they understand how they can uphold those values? And what are we doing to help the individuals who have been with us for years stay aligned with those values?

Unfortunately, I've seen far too many scenarios where team members aren't even provided with clarity about how their work aligns with performance metrics. If that's unclear, I doubt they'd have much chance of tying any of it to the organization's values.

"Doing Good" but What Does Good Look Like?

I started my first full-time job just after turning fifteen, and, as they say, the rest is history. But that history makes for a good story every now and then! In this case, the story won't be particularly amusing. Still, it's certainly relevant to why it's so vital for us to remove the ambiguity that too often surrounds our core values and can just as often keep our team members from understanding how the work they're performing connects directly with the compensation they receive.

Over the years, I've worked with supervisors, managers, and business owners to improve or implement formal performance review processes, providing team members with specific feedback on their performance in their roles. I don't recall ever receiving an evaluation of any kind until approximately 90 days into my first job in manufacturing, nearly five years after I joined the workforce. That may be because my first job at fifteen was just for the summer or because several of the positions I held over the next few years were with small companies.

Even while working for a large grocery store chain during my last two years of high school, I don't recall ever sitting down with a manager to receive input on how I was doing. That could have been because I took on new positions within the company as quickly as I was able to earn them, and those "promotions" were what they considered as reviews, or it could be because I spent most of my time away from work and school doing all I could to cull my weaker brain cells… Either way, I was left to assume that the effort I put into my job was what my bosses expected since they allowed me to continue showing up, and I kept receiving a paycheck for it.

> **I was left to assume that the effort I put into my job was what my bosses expected since they allowed me to continue showing up.**

That first real review in the manufacturing facility was intimidating. I had been through for around three months and was one of the youngest people in the building. The company employed a stepped pay grade system, and missing out on a bump to the next step would extend the time it took to reach the top of the pay scale by around six months, which would typically take around five years in the best-case scenario at the time. I remember my supervisor reviewing the single sheet of paper he had prepared in advance, pointing to the dozen or so bubbles he had filled in and telling me which ones meant that I exceeded requirements, met requirements, or needed improvement.

That took him all of about a minute. I don't recall much about that, but I'm sure the "exceeds requirements" marks were scarce. Being so new to the manufacturing world, I was still trying to figure things out. On the next payday, however, I saw a slight increase in my hourly rate—but I had no idea how I had earned it.

The decade and a half that followed wasn't much different. I received "raises" on schedule and had plenty of opportunities to take on new roles. However, I still don't recall a single review where I was told how any specific tasks I performed made a direct contribution to the organization's goals or what I could do differently to achieve better results. While that changed slightly when I moved from an hourly role to a salaried position, the feedback was still abstract and tied more to big-picture metrics that my work had little (if any) impact on.

Even once I was in a human resources role within that large company, there wasn't much I could do to change this. But when I took a position with a smaller company, I had the chance to help provide the team members being evaluated with something I had gotten very little of through over two decades of employment: direct input on how their effort tied to the results we achieved as a company! I was excited about this because I never got much value from hearing that I was doing good when I didn't have a clear picture of what "good" looked like, or what it would take to go from good to great. Just like providing feedback after a behavior-based safety observation, this required me and the supervisor or manager leading the review to be familiar with the actions the team member had taken, and be competent enough with their role so we could explain how those actions contributed to or took away from that oh-so-necessary productivity. With this kind of specificity, even a dreaded "needs improvement" mark provided valuable insight.

I'll bet you can relate to some aspect of this. Hopefully, it's the latter, but I'm guessing you've experienced the former at some point in your career, too. If you have any involvement in providing evaluations for team members you work with, which example would they connect with most? In my experience, I've seen far too many who only see which dots are filled in without understanding why. And if they don't know how their performance led to or prevented a pay increase, what are the odds of them having any real idea how they're supposed to be living out a set of values printed in a handbook, or painted on the wall? We've got to remove that ambiguity!

Providing Specific Examples

Before we walk through a few steps we can take to remove every bit of ambiguity possible, let's tackle an issue every leader faces at one point or another: even when we detail exactly what "doing good" looks like for each of our team members, it can still be tough to address performance that just isn't meeting expectations. In many cases, a minor issue is completely overlooked, time and again, simply because addressing it directly seems more difficult than working around the problem. While I know I've been guilty of this too, choosing this path only reinforces the less-than-desirable behavior, compounding what we'll inevitably need to deal with down the road.

Not long after I started what turned out to be my last full-time position before transitioning to self-employment, I worked directly with the owner of that company (who was my immediate supervisor) to implement a more concise performance evaluation process. While the one-page sheet I had suggested was streamlined from the five-page report the company had in place but rarely used, the key to it providing any measurable value was based on the specific details surrounding each topic it addressed.

Since I was somewhere between 60 and 90 days into my role with the company, I suggested he use me as his guinea pig. The first section addressed "Job Knowledge," and he rated me as "Meets Requirements." Before he could even provide any details, I told him I disagreed with him. He looked a little puzzled but quickly offered to change it to "Exceeds Requirements." For perspective, I had been in safety and human resources for around fifteen years at that point and had dealt with close to ten times the number of employees in other roles. That said, the bulk of my experience was in a very different industry, and I had a ton to learn to perform at the level I wanted for his organization. I explained that I thought "Needs Improvement" was a much more realistic rating, and detailed the areas I knew I needed to grow in.

I don't share that story to criticize the owner of that company (I truly enjoyed working with him) but as an example of how daunting it can be to provide what the other person may receive as criticism. In *Know What You're FOR*[13], Jeff Henderson quotes Dr. Tim Irwin as providing an alternative approach: "Alliance Feedback is where a manager aligns herself with the employee, helping them live out who they truly want to become." Henderson goes on to compare the two seemingly similar ideas by saying, "Constructive criticism is top-down. Alliance Feedback is peer-to-peer."

> **"Alliance Feedback is where a manager aligns herself with the employee, helping them live out who they truly want to become."**

I realize performance reviews are, indeed, top-down, but there's no requirement for a supervisor or manager to treat their team members as minions; we most certainly can build strong relationships and work with them as peers. Having different responsibilities or job titles doesn't mean either role is any more important than the other.

When I pushed back on the "Meets Requirements" rating, I knew enough about the position I was in to have a clear understanding of the gaps I still needed to fill to provide what he needed from me in that organization. That's why it made sense for me to be the guinea pig for that new evaluation approach. The tweak we were able to make from then on was to provide specific details for each team member being reviewed, covering exactly how their performance exceeded requirements, met requirements, or needed improvement based on where they were in the pay scale for their current role AND we were able to provide Alliance Feedback (although we didn't call it that then because I'd hadn't met Jeff Henderson yet) on what they needed to work on to reach their next goal.

When we only provide general feedback, whether it's approval or constructive criticism, we leave our team members to fill in the blanks on how each particular action they're taking ties in. The same thing happens when we've only listed our values in the policy manual (that nobody ever actually looks at anyway) or somewhere on the wall in our office. Even the most articulate definition can be tough to connect with each role. Just as specifics matter in the performance review process, this kind of clarity about how each value ties to the work each of us does can prevent things from going wrong, as in the scenario we examined earlier.

Behavioral Examples That Define Our Values

We've looked at how things can go *really* wrong without strong organizational values in place, and how easy it can be to fall short of providing a picture of those values for everyone on our teams. We've also dug into how, even with specific values listed in various places throughout our office, we can't assume everyone will have the same level of understanding. And to show just how often we provide our folks with feedback that lacks the detail they need to improve subpar performance or repeat what they're doing well, I challenged you to think about the evaluations you've received (or given) that didn't include a single example of actual behavior. While each of these is common, providing solid behavioral examples that define our values doesn't have to be this way! It's not complicated, and it doesn't require us to transform into some sort of superhero. All we need to do is provide a visible example, and share it consistently with our teams.

Make no mistake: I believe this is something each of us can build into our daily routines fairly simply. That said, I'm certainly not suggesting it will be *easy*. The challenge is to know what *WE* need to do to live out those values. It's one thing to memorize the words or even spout off the definitions occasionally, but knowing exactly how we exemplify them through our own behavior requires us to become more intimate with our core values than simply stating them in front of a group. Quite honestly, putting intentional thought into how our behaviors model our values should be the most challenging part of the process. As leaders, we likely have the most discretion in how we executive the tasks we're responsible for—and, indeed, how we've decided to take that action is in line with what we've defined as our values.

> **Knowing exactly how we exemplify them through our own behavior requires us to become more intimate with our core values.**

With those dots connected, our next step should fall right in line: we need to be sure we're explaining why we do what we do. Hold tight, though; this ain't about bragging about ourselves. It's about making (and keeping) our values part of our team's regular conversations. A few years ago, when a good friend of ours served as general manager for a heavy equipment company, he helped his team adopt a mantra of "Customers for Life." Each time someone in the office asked for help, the coworker assisting would provide them with what they needed and repeat the phrase for everyone to hear. When a customer called for support, one of the first things you'd hear after the call ended was the team member sharing, "Customers for Life," as they hung up the phone.

In leading our teams, we have opportunities each day to build our values into our conversations. When we tie those values to actions we're taking, we've started the process of providing behavioral examples that define our core values.

With this as a starting point, our next step should be detailing how the work our team members are doing connects to those values.

Make It About Values, Not Us...

Highlighting our own behavior to provide examples that define our values certainly helps us build those values into the conversations we have with our teams, but don't mistake this as a suggestion to be boastful about how amazing we are; it's anything but that!

Not long after starting our business, Cindy and I led a small group through an extensive study of John Maxwell's book *Everyone Communicates, Few Connect*. Following nearly every idea we discussed as a group, one participant asked what would keep someone from using it to manipulate others. After talking through this at least half a dozen times, I couldn't take any more. Truth be told, I had never considered using anything we were covering with the group to take advantage of someone. If you're even remotely familiar with Maxwell's work, you know that's definitely not something he'd ever so much as imply. My *final* response was something like, "The only ones who would use this to be manipulative are the ones who are just plain manipulative!" That was the last it was brought up. I had clearly pissed off that participant, and I no longer cared!

What I learned through dealing with that participant over the year or so that followed was that they were very willing to spin things in a way that would manipulate a situation for their own benefit, and apparently very suspicious that others were just as willing to reciprocate. If our approach to highlighting our own behaviors as examples for defining our values is to shine a light on ourselves and manipulate our teams for personal gain, then we probably have more folks complying with us because they *have* to rather than people following us because they *want* to. However, when sharing those examples serves as a foundation that'll benefit our team members even more than it benefits us, they'll be far more receptive when we work to explain how their behaviors align with those same core values.

In so many of the organizations we've worked for (and with) over the years, Cindy and I have seen incredibly skilled team members be promoted to supervisory and management roles—and they've earned those promotions! That was the main reason we created our *Emerging Leader Development* course: to help bridge the gap between their technical expertise and the skills they needed to *lead* their teams as effectively as they'd achieved results on their own. But even the ones with the broadest technical experience had rarely mastered every single role they'd be responsible for managing in their new position. In some cases, we saw supervisors and managers take on responsibility for positions they had no personal experience in. As we take on more and more responsibilities as leaders, a harsh reality we must face is that we won't always be the best at every task that needs to be done—and it's not reasonable to expect ourselves to be. That said, we will need to become competent in everything we're charged with overseeing. When we accomplish that—by learning the behaviors necessary to complete each task successfully—we can tie our organization's core values to those behaviors in nearly any conversation we have with our teams, whether individually or in group settings.

While this may sound daunting at first, that's not my intent. As we're intentional about starting this process, it can become part of our routine over time. It will likely be awkward at first and tough to remember at times, but eventually, we can develop it into a habit. In addition to tying behaviors to values in our general conversations, we also need to ensure this is a focal point in each of our formal discussions with our teams.

A Part of Every Conversation

We don't need an elaborate, "official" presentation to illustrate our core values. It's far more critical that we exemplify the appropriate behaviors personally, and that we recognize our team members for doing so in their roles. While implementing either of these practices may feel overwhelming initially, consistency matters far more than how flashy the rollout is. In *The 15 Invaluable Laws of Growth*, John Maxwell says this about the value of being consistent: "The sooner you make the transition to becoming intentional about your personal growth, the better it will be for you, because growth compounds and accelerates if you remain intentional about it.[14]" I'm very willing to make the same argument for being consistent in talking about and modeling our values; it will indeed compound and accelerate when you're intentional about it!

By using our own examples in conversations occasionally and working to applaud our team members for exemplifying values in our routine interaction with them, we're laying a solid foundation for the role those values play in the organization. Our next step should be weaving our values into every formal conversation we have with our teams.

Earlier, I shared how much value comes from providing specific examples during a performance evaluation rather than simply pointing to the dot we've filled in, showing "meets requirements." As we detail the behaviors we've observed them using that led to the score we've given them, we have an excellent opportunity to tie those behaviors back to our company's core values. Whether their work exceeded, met, or fell short of requirements, we'd do well to connect their action to a specific value and explain how they're living up to or falling short of that value. If we've consistently discussed our values in general conversations, this may become a natural part of our conversation.

One last but critical place where we need to be intentional about discussing our values is during any corrective action conversation. I realize these are difficult discussions for every leader, mainly because leaders care about the people they're responsible for. But speaking to how the behaviors calling for this type of conversation are not aligned with our values, while providing detail showing what the expected change needs to look like, can go a long way toward actually *correcting* the action instead of only being a punitive measure. As I detailed in *What's KILLING Your Profitability?*, turnover is far too expensive not to do all we can to help someone change when possible.

I don't suggest any of this will be easy or will magically fall into place overnight. However, as we take small, consistent steps to provide detailed examples so that everyone on our team knows and understands what's involved (and expected) with living out our values, we'll remove that costly ambiguity and be closer to having a strong foundation for our organization to grow from. And that will help us avoid issues in nearly every area of our business. We'll examine some of those next to emphasize how important it is to ensure our values are more than just words in the handbook.

CHAPTER FOUR

WHO REALLY CARES ABOUT YOUR VALUES?
YOUR TEAM DOES!

Let's assume your organization has done a solid job of articulating what your values mean and has worked to remove all possible ambiguity by connecting those values to the daily activities of each team member. Then, what? As leaders, the ball most definitely remains in our court.

An Inc.com article called "9 Ways to Reinforce and Live Your Company's Core Values Everyday[15]" had this at the top of the list:

> Live and lead by example. Leaders are always being watched. Setting core values, and then failing to abide by them, is worse than not establishing core values at all. A solid core values system is especially important in difficult times. It's rather easy to adhere to established desired behaviors when things are going well. When a company hits a bump in the road however, is when it's most important to stand by what you believe at your core.

Regardless of where you are in your organization, you've accepted some level of leadership responsibility; I can't imagine you'd be on this journey with me otherwise. But before I challenge you to take a hard look at the example you're providing anyone you've earned influence with, I want you to consider who really cares about your values. Spoiler alert: your team does! That said, the folks looking to you for leadership are no different than you and me.

Throughout *What's KILLING Your Profitability? (It ALL Boils Down to Leadership!)*, and a few times in *Leading With A Clear Purpose*, I shared this from a Harvard Business Review article called "Things They Do for Love[16]":

"Company leaders won't be surprised that employee engagement—the extent to which workers commit to something or someone in their organizations—influences performance and retention. But they may be surprised by how much engagement matters. Increased commitment can lead to a 57% improvement in discretionary effort— that is, employees' willingness to exceed duty's call. That greater effort produces, on average, a 20% individual performance improvement and an 87% reduction in the desire to pull up stakes."

Having shared these statistics with groups across the United States for a few years now, I've seen more than a few wrinkled foreheads and scowls as folks wrap their heads around the idea of 57% additional discretionary effort and the 20% uptick in individual productivity. I counter those looks of disbelief with the same question I need you to answer right now: who have you worked the hardest for, or been the most committed to throughout your career? The supervisor who ruled with an iron fist, or the one you knew had your best interests at heart in every way?

Since I know your answer, let's consider how the behaviors of the individual who earned our increased discretionary effort aligned with the core values of the organization we were part of, as well as our personal values. For me, it comes back to this simple statement in an article from Lesley University titled "The Power of Company Core Values[17]," which references the importance of leading by example: "Seeing leaders adhere to the same principles they enforce is crucial for building trust and cohesion."

During an orientation session I led more than a decade ago, my boss at the time was speaking with a new team member we had just hired. This gentleman was joining the company with an exceptional set of skills, but he was new to the area, so we knew it would take time for the team to welcome him.

My boss told him, "You'll build a thousand bridges before you're ever known as a bridge builder. But if you (expletive) just one donkey, you'll be forever known as a donkey (expletive-er)." Having recently left a very formal corporate environment, that statement nearly knocked me out of my chair—but it couldn't have been more accurate. Trust is indeed earned over time, and can be lost in an instant. Trust is the foundation for earning influence and engagement, which in turn leads to increased discretionary effort and individual productivity.

Since that's something so critical for both of us, isn't it fair to think our teams are looking for the same from us?

Earning Our Team's Trust

Since I had no direct authority over the team of behavior-based safety observers who supported me for more than a decade, earning and maintaining their trust was a crucial part of why they chose to remain engaged in the process when it would have been easier for each of them to focus solely on their actual job requirements.

To that end, I had to be just as careful about being credible with everyone else in the facility. During my nearly twenty years in manufacturing, I can recall only two instances where I went on the shop floor without wearing safety glasses. In each case, I had my regular glasses on and forgot to swap them out. I can think of only one time when I didn't stop to put on steel-toe shoes before entering a production area, and that was when I was called in late one night to begin an accident investigation.

I'm not making excuses for any of these, but sharing how intentional I was about setting the best example I could, because I knew everyone would be watching me—I couldn't expect anyone to take my input on how their behavior could put them at risk if I weren't following the company's safety guidelines. As my former boss shared in his example, trust can be lost very quickly!

When it comes to our core values, we can have the clearest words and most articulate definitions in place. Still, our teams will pay far more attention to what we do than to anything they see on paper, or a single word we say about those values in a company meeting.

A few years ago, a friend (who happened to be one of the top performers in his organization) shared that the executive team in the company he worked for had recently implemented a policy defining how quickly team members were expected to respond to customers and clients. His concern was that he had sent several requests to two individuals on the executive team, all of which had gone well beyond the time defined in the policy, with no acknowledgment whatsoever. Near the end of *When: The Scientific Secrets of Perfect Timing*[18], Daniel Pink cites research by Duncan Watts, a Columbia University sociologist and principal researcher for Microsoft Research, who stated, "Email response time is the single best predictor of whether the employees are satisfied with their boss. The longer it takes for a boss to respond to their emails, the less satisfied people are with their leader."

If those executives were attempting to hold responsiveness up as one of the company's core values, were they succeeding in exemplifying it to their team? Before you assume that their lack of response was an isolated instance, I'll share something we learned (I believe from Mark Cole, CEO of Maxwell Leadership and closing keynote at our 2025 LeadershipLegacy Experience): "How we do one thing is how we do everything!" Would it come as a surprise to learn that my friend is no longer with that organization?

With the importance of earning and maintaining trust being fresh in our minds, let's imagine teamwork is a core value of your company. Simple enough, huh? I can't imagine an organization that wouldn't want to strive to model world-class teamwork. If the executive team defines that as "building on trust" while developing business relationships with out-of-town partners that actively undermine long-standing local relationships, especially when preaching to their employees and customers about enriching their community, what are the chances that team members will begin questioning the character of those executives? You and I both know the answer.

Certainly, leadership is not easy. In fact, it's damn hard! A friend of mine shares a phrase heard often at West Point: "choosing the harder right over the easier wrong." When it comes to earning and maintaining buy-in from our team, exemplifying our values will require choosing the harder right. If it's not important enough to do so, are they our values—or just words we're hoping to impress people with? We'll dig into that more soon. First, though, let's examine what we can expect if we fail to exemplify and uphold our stated values.

If We Fail to Lead by Example...

As I shared what I've observed personally over the last several years for what I believe is a textbook example of using core values as a foundation for an organization, I mentioned how I've seen Craig and Kim work to ensure every member of their team understands exactly what each value looks like in their daily routine. This provides not just the written definition, but a behavioral example of how each value applies in various scenarios. While the overall revenue has grown substantially since they acquired their business, a company that had already been in operation for three-quarters of a century, that isn't the most remarkable part of the equation. Watching their team grow exponentially more cohesive as they work to live out those values has been nothing short of amazing!

Throughout my three-plus decades in the workforce, I've witnessed numerous organizations undergo changes in management, including both globally operating companies and locally owned and operated ones. Except in cases where the person taking the reins had an existing presence in the company, leadership changes were often closely tied to changes in personnel at multiple other levels.

Despite this being the norm, that was not what Craig and Kim experienced with their new team. Quite honestly, the only thing I can attribute to the surprising level of stability during a complete transition of ownership (not just management) is their commitment to living up to their stated values.

Before we work through steps for doing this ourselves, we need to consider the alternative we'll inevitably have to deal with if we don't. Reflect on how exemplifying our values helps us earn trust with each of our team members. More importantly, think about how the inverse is just as true! While the best performers in our organizations may not push the clutch in entirely when they see us do something that doesn't align with our core values, such as preaching the importance of doing business locally while actively forming alliances with out-of-towners, it will most definitely catch their attention. And if they encounter more things over time that create doubt, we can expect to lose at least a portion of their discretionary effort. Top performers will always fulfill what their job requires, but they may be less willing to go above and beyond.

Sooner or later, though, that disconnect between our behaviors and what we hold up as our values will prompt those who have high standards to seek another place to call home. How can we blame them? Remember my friend who couldn't get a response from the executives who expected him to reply within 48 hours? It took a few years, but he started his own business when he could no longer follow those who wouldn't lead by example.

With that cautionary tale in mind, the next thing we need to focus on is what we can do to build a team around a strong set of values we are willing to live by.

Rallying Your Team Around Your Values

As I opened the second section of *Leading With A Clear Purpose*, I shared the story of my fondest Major League Baseball memory, the 2004 American League Championship Series, where the Boston Red Sox narrowly avoided being swept and came back to win four straight games against the New York Yankees before winning four more in a row against the St Louis Cardinals to win their first World Series since 1918. As much as I enjoyed the Red Sox making history (and knocking out the Yankees while doing so), the point I made was regarding the immense talent on that New York roster.

On paper, it didn't seem like Boston stood a chance of coming back when they were down in Game 4, let alone to win the series. For the purposes of *Leading With A Clear Purpose*, I emphasized how it's not always just about the pay; a clear and definite purpose can be what drives mediocre talent to outperform some of the best in any industry. When it comes to our core values, that is precisely what our team needs to see in action to come together. If we haven't been intentional about providing our team with a consistent example of precisely what our core values look like in practice, having even the most talented individuals throughout our organization won't yield a cohesive team.

> **A clear and definite purpose can be what drives mediocre talent to outperform some of the best in any industry.**

Can You Build a Great Team Without Values?

I recall an announcer commenting on the 2004 American League Championship Series that the Yankees had one of the best rosters he had ever seen on paper. His counterpart responded that the Red Sox players showed up to finish the series on the field. Not only did I enjoy his sarcastic jab at the Yankees, but I also loved his point that a group of people choosing to work as a team can perform significantly better than even the most talented individuals working independently near one another.

Think back to how things can go really wrong in an organization, whether we have articulate definitions for each value or not when the people counting on us for leadership don't see us deliberately walking our talk. Even if we're fortunate enough to keep the talent on our roster, it's improbable that the individuals with that talent will have a reason to rally around a common goal. Without values serving as a foundation, those talented team members may expend more energy competing against one another than collaborating with each other.

> **Without values serving as a foundation, those talented team members may expend more energy competing against one another than collaborating with each other.**

No Good Reason for Compromising Our Values

I'll say it again: even the most talented individuals rarely form a great team without clear, foundational values. For more than two decades, I've heard John Maxwell emphasize how "everything rises and falls on leadership." When it comes to building a foundation on those values, those of us who accept the responsibility that comes with each of the most senior roles in our organizations will indeed be viewed as leaders—whether we've earned true influence with the team reporting to us or not. Our actions in those leadership roles most definitely set the tone for the behavior of each individual, which in turn determines what we have around us: a cohesive team or a group of individual performers looking out for their own best interests.

> **The most senior roles in our organizations will indeed be viewed as leaders—whether we've earned true influence with the team reporting to us or not.**

I can't think of an organization that doesn't place at least some level of priority on integrity, even if that's not one of the core values painted on the wall. If we define that as doing the right thing, no matter what, but make decisions that directly conflict with that out of fear that a competitor may sneak in to take some of our business, how are our most motivated employees likely to follow suit? Let's be honest: people do what people see. In every for-profit business I've ever seen, there's a significant need to acquire and retain customers; that's how the lights stay on.

Suppose an executive twists the definition of integrity to justify how they've staved off potential competition while subtly crossing the line on what they've held up as an integrous business practice. In that case, many folks reporting to them will see that as permission to push the envelope even more. While there will always be some people in the organization who will take the high road, regardless of any executive's example, their level of commitment to engaging with the rest of the team will drop off over time.

All organizations, including those in government, have a responsibility to provide service to their customers and clients. As a quick side note, I suppose one could argue that most government organizations seem to view service more in veterinary terms (if you catch my drift). If we claim to prioritize others, but our leadership decisions are routinely based on what makes us look best while directly or indirectly undermining our partners, is it reasonable to expect others in our organization to follow suit? We both know the answer to that as well.

In an environment where individual performance is incentivized, even the most innocent cases of tip-toeing around what we point to as our core values to justify choosing the easy wrong over the harder right serve as permission for everyone else to wiggle the definitions around as they need to fit their actions, especially when those actions yield immediate financial return. That kind of culture certainly attracts high performers who are willing to do anything for a buck, but it will not build a high-performing team that consistently delivers results in the long term. Even the slightest variances from our values, especially when exemplified by those in leadership roles, will erode any hope of creating a cohesive team. It's what Simon Sinek referred to in *The Infinite Game* as "an infection that festers over time."

Before working through precisely what we need to do so our values help build a great team with top-tier talent, we need to have a clear picture of how talent alone doesn't guarantee organizational results.

The Best Talent Doesn't Equal the Best Team

Whether it's because we've compromised our values, losing credibility with some of the best folks who had previously carried our team, or we simply didn't put enough intentional effort into rallying everyone around a clearly articulated set of core values, the highest performers in our organizations will find a way to be part of a culture that lives out the values painted on the wall or listed in the handbook. In most cases, those folks are direct targets for our competition to lure away. But sometimes, the disconnect between what's listed as an organizational value and what's seen daily is all an incredibly talented employee needs to take a stab at starting their own business. In either case, a company that previously had some of the most skilled people in their field can find themselves ill-equipped to maintain a long-standing reputation.

> **The highest performers in our organizations will find a way to be part of a culture that lives out the values.**

I often share how I hired 225 employees during the last eighteen months I worked for a large manufacturing company and how that only increased the overall headcount by about twenty. At that point, we were using every option we could find to identify potential candidates, and very few of those came through referrals from current employees.

Just a few years before that, though, and for all the preceding years I was with that organization, employee referrals were the primary source. While that facility experienced several management changes in a short period, that wasn't the most significant factor behind those referrals drying up. The more pressing issue was that the managers calling the shots at that point didn't align with the values shared by many of the longest-tenured (and most loyal) employees. That, and the fact that those managers never invested much energy in building relationships with employees so that anyone would have had an understanding of what they valued, played a significant part in the recruitment and retention process for that company. And the folks who remained had little reason to form a tight-knit team.

Another example I've watched unfold over the years was a smaller organization that once had a world-class team. Each department head, and many key contributors throughout the company, were truly the best in their respective areas. While the executive team in that organization didn't necessarily compromise their stated values, they just didn't place enough emphasis on them to provide the best employees with a reason to collaborate actively. In most cases, this only resulted in apathy, but there were a few occasions where some of the best on the roster were actively competing against each other for jobs and positions within the company.

While all organizations have some level of turnover, even if that's just due to retirements, losing extremely talented people is never easy to absorb. Not only did retirements have a bit of an impact, but no less than six of those outstanding performers—several of whom had been with the company for many years—started their own businesses, actively competing with their old company.

I'll never pretend that simply listing a few words and definitions on the wall or in a handbook is all it takes to build a great team. Still, I've never seen a talented group of people work cohesively over a long period without having a strong foundation of values that are meaningful to them all.

With that in mind, our next step will be to work through specific actions we can all take to rally our teams around the core values of our organization.

Great Results Come From Great Teams

Having looked at how much folks within our organizations need us to exemplify what we're holding up as core values, and detailing how unlikely we are to build a great team without those values being a legitimate part of what we're doing daily, let's dig into some practical steps each of us should be doing to rally our team around our company values.

I'd love to cite several articles referencing mounds of data that show global companies with monstrous growth simply because their executives backed their value talk with a disciplined value walk, breaking records year after year. I searched for it and found plenty of articles listing the big names we'd all expect to read about, but I've seen just as many articles bashing those same companies for less than scrupulous practices.

That being the case, let's stick with some that I have very close proximity with. As I explained, the textbook example I saw my friends provide for each of the five values they used as the foundation for the business they acquired in 2021, I shared some of the growth that the business recognized during the first twenty-four months it was owned, as well as a few things they've since achieved. With now four separate businesses under the parent company they've formed, all based on those same five values, the cohesion is nothing short of amazing. Not only has the first business grown substantially, but the others are following suit as well. Every time I talk with Craig, which is at least once each week, he tells me about an excellent new client or a new opportunity that's as big as any they've had to date. None of that is a coincidence. I see nearly every member of his team firing on all cylinders to support this growth. Not only is the existing team actively engaged, but they've also made some outstanding additions.

I once heard Jack Welch say that even the best managers only make the right hire about 50% of the time. Having been involved in well over a thousand hiring decisions, I'm far too familiar with why he made that statement. Even the most thorough interviews are rarely long enough to learn everything you need to know about a candidate's work history or existing skill set.

With all the employment law rules and regulations surrounding what can and cannot be discussed during an interview, it can be challenging to get a complete picture of who the person really is. In many cases, the leaders most experienced in the hiring process use their intuition to determine if the candidate with a reasonable level of competency will actually fit in with the rest of the existing team. Sometimes, all this works out wonderfully, and sometimes, the person who shows up for their first day of work looks and sounds like the person you interviewed yet acts completely different right from the start.

The most resounding thing I've seen come from the strong foundation Craig and Kim have built across all their companies by consistently modeling their core values is how much the overall impact has spilled over into the hiring process. Since they've experienced so little voluntary turnover, and much of what they have had has been through planned retirements, they've had the luxury of being very intentional about screening every candidate. Relevant skills certainly play a role, but every aspect of how the person connects with the existing team ties into the final decision. Since they're also building a very positive reputation—resulting in multiple quality candidates applying for each position that's posted—the team has grown stronger through nearly every hire. Great results indeed come from great teams, and those great teams rally around great values that their leaders model daily.

Great Teams Are Built On Great Values

For the casual observer, it may appear that the results each of the businesses Craig and Kim have acquired are the primary reasons so many solid candidates have applied to join their team. After all, who doesn't want to be part of a winning team?

Where I'd challenge that casual observer, though, lies in determining what had to be in place first. This is most definitely not a chicken-or-egg scenario! Had they not initially solidified a foundation based on their five core values, I'm convinced the results would have been vastly different. I believe turnover would have been much closer to the national average, if not even higher since management changes nearly always result in a spike in personnel changes. Simply maintaining the existing client base would have proven to be a challenge, too, with a lot of different faces in place.

Great results unquestionably come from great teams, especially those that are sustained over long periods. A company with many talented individuals can also produce strong results in any given year when there are enough incentives in place. Still, there's a tremendous difference between several people achieving individual results and an entire team consistently performing exceptionally well. If teamwork is held up as a value, and defined with the idea of building on trust, the most effective individual performers will produce on their own but, if they see an executive making decisions out of fear that undermine the community they're professing to serve, they'll have little reason to look for ways to collaborate with the surrounding team. When each of the folks watching Craig and Kim saw them routinely making decisions that benefited everyone involved—even when doing so cost them personally at the moment—it didn't take long for the most talented folks on the team to look for ways they could support not just the new owners, but everyone around them.

Had those values been just words printed in a handbook or painted on the wall, the existing team members wouldn't have had a reason to rally around a couple who had little industry knowledge, and that would have had a direct impact on the caliber of candidates who were willing to accept positions in the company. The name of the business had been in place for more than seven decades, but basing each decision on those values created a foundation for the new owners to build on moving forward.

If this were the only example I've seen, I probably wouldn't be as adamant about how much those values contributed to building their (now extremely) strong team. In complete transparency, we've seen at least a dozen other clients experience results like this. I've been referencing Craig and Kim here because I've had the opportunity to be on the journey with them every step of the way. Another friend's business has grown exponentially in the decade he's owned it, going from ten employees to over fifty. He has held a similar set of core company values as a foundation throughout it all. He's passed on highly skilled candidates (at times when he had a pressing need for their credentials) because those candidates had reputations that contradicted his organization's values.

Another friend holds a leadership role in public safety. While nearly all the other localities are constantly recruiting, he cultivates a waitlist of top-notch candidates before he ever posts an open position. Interestingly enough, the locality he presides over also has far less public drama and a substantially better working relationship with local businesses than any other in our area. How he's established and built his team around a core set of values has played a critical role in that.

When we're willing to do the work upfront to ensure our core values are truly what we're building our team around, the excellent results aren't limited to the company's bottom line. Those values will show through in everything our team does for the communities and clients we serve. Before we begin looking at how our values impact anyone outside our organizations, though, let's close the loop with why those values give our team members a reason to look beyond the results they achieve for themselves.

Great Values Show Up in Everything We Do

Throughout *Leading With A Clear Purpose*, I emphasized how important it is for everyone in a leadership role to understand precisely why they do what they do, to share a message with our teams detailing why our organization exists, and to help each team member understand their own purpose while connecting it back to what we're working toward as a company. As critical as that clear purpose is, making a meaningful impact—individually or as part of a great team— truly does rely on having and living a great set of core values.

As we lead our teams, how we choose to live out what we list as our core business values will eventually be reflected in everything our team does, with exponential results—positive or negative. During the time I've known Craig and Kim, most of my interactions have been with Craig. Through all that, I've witnessed numerous examples of how he exemplifies their core value of Integrity, both in his interactions with the team and in his responses to customers and clients. When he and I discussed their list of core values initially, he considered adding "Profitability" as a sixth value. After considering it further, he decided that upholding each of the others— especially Integrity—would yield a level of profitability that may never be achieved by simply including it in the handbook. Since then, this has undoubtedly proven the case.

> **How we choose to live out what we list as our core business values will eventually be reflected in everything our team does, with exponential results.**

However, many of his choices to model integrity cut into profitability on the front end. Providing replacement products and services beyond a warranty, offering refunds in times when the business was in the right, and even choosing the high road when a non-profit took advantage of his goodwill. Not only were his team members watching closely, they were able to begin replicating this in their own roles. They truly did rally around Craig's example of Integrity, as well as the other four values he (and Kim) displayed daily. Those values began to show up in what everyone did: first, the key team members, then nearly everyone in the organization.

With Integrity being something many organizations list as a core value, though, you and I both know that all executives aren't willing to back their talk with the same intentional walk. Have you ever worked for someone who expected you to perform in a certain way but consistently missed the mark in doing so themselves, then justified it by detailing why their busyness was an acceptable reason while *your* busyness was not? If Integrity is as simple as just doing the right thing, what are the odds of that type of justification being replicated and viewed as "the right thing" at every other level of the organization?

Unfortunately, we've all seen examples like that far more often than we've seen a Craig— someone who lives the values he holds in front of his team daily, and is the first to accept responsibility for an issue, regardless of where it originated.

While the examples I've shared here, good and bad, have been brief and vague, I'd challenge you to think through the values in your organization. How have you seen them modeled by leaders? How are you exemplifying them for the team looking to you for leadership? And how are those values showing through in everything your team does? What we have listed won't mean nearly as much as what people see in our behavior. Over time, that behavior will create a lasting impact on the clients and communities we serve—so that's what we'll work through next!

CHAPTER FIVE

WHO ELSE CARES ABOUT YOUR VALUES?
YOUR CLIENTS & COMMUNITY DO!

A great team will definitely care about the core values we exemplify as we build the foundation for our organization, but that's not where the importance of those values stops. How leaders (as well as each team member) live out those values will impact business relationships with individual clients and the communities in which the business operates. When it comes to what clients and the surrounding community see, the owners and executives won't be the only ones providing the example. Realistically, every member of our team is part of our marketing department when it comes to displaying our core values.

In sharing how we can rally our team around a strong set of values, I mentioned a friend in public safety who typically has a list of candidates asking to join his team each time he posts an open position. Since he's in law enforcement, let's consider how much negative publicity that entire community receives when *any* police officer—anywhere in the country—is so much as portrayed as having used poor judgment, let alone breaking one of the laws they've sworn to uphold. Each time this happens, it casts a shadow on everyone wearing a uniform, whatever the location or facts.

Whether we like it or not, the same principle applies to how each member of our organization represents our brand. While price is undoubtedly *a factor*—and one that has made plenty of headlines because of the crazy inflation we've all dealt with in recent years—it's not always *the primary factor* in winning and retaining business. The organizational values we live by, and how each of our team members displays those values in and out of work, play a critical role in earning and maintaining trust from our clients and the communities we're part of—even when we're not attempting to compete solely on price.

I frequently make this case with the companies Cindy and I support that have technicians servicing clients' equipment. Many of those clients rarely, if ever, interact with the organization's executive team. Sometimes they have occasional conversations with the person responsible for sales or business development. However, the majority of clients' opinions of these companies are formed through what they see and hear from the individual performing the work at their location. Those technicians generally have excellent technical skills, but how they display their core values (through their speech and behavior) often provides the client with all they need to form an opinion.

Another way our company values are reflected in our interactions with clients and the community lies in who and what we support. Not so long ago, a friend who manages a great local company shared a social media post about who sponsors Little League teams. We don't see Amazon or Walmart on those jerseys, but we do see the names of local businesses where we know people personally. That same friend has been very intentional about how his company contributes to community initiatives, especially those closely aligned with their business model. While they do indeed provide products and services that are priced very competitively with their competition, the organization has developed an extremely loyal client base by backing their values with action. The leadership team and each public-facing team member consistently provide reasons for the people they serve to like and trust them. And when all things are equal, we'd all prefer to do business with someone we know, like, and trust.

How Values Impact "Know, Like, & Trust" Relationships

Let's set aside any leadership responsibilities we hold for a moment and consider how much an organization's values—specifically, how each team member upholds or fails to uphold those values—impact our desire to do business with them. As regular joes, clients, or even just members of the community where a particular company operates, does the example each of those team members set affect how well we know them, how much we like them, and how much we trust them?

For me, the answer is a resounding *yes*. In wrapping up part one of *Leading With A Clear Purpose*, I shared the stated purpose behind those (in)famous golden arches—and how much variance there was when I last attempted to order what vaguely resembled fast food from one of their restaurants about two hours away from home. It's been several years since then, and I still have a very clear picture in my mind of how the behaviors we observed contradicted the organization's stated purpose and values. Interestingly enough, society often overlooks missteps from employees in a large company like that while dropping a small business like a bad habit for anything remotely similar.

> **I still have a very clear picture in my mind of how the behaviors we observed contradicted the organization's stated purpose and values.**

That difference, it seems, is almost always driven by the sheer convenience provided by the bigger ones, or maybe just a lack of willingness to take a stand on principle. Either way, employees (at any level) who fail to live up to their company's values send a distinct message to their customers and the community they're part of.

We've all heard the saying, "We do business with people we know, like, and trust." I was introduced to this idea more than two decades ago, and I've always viewed it as a fundamental truth in business relationships. As we've worked with and studied the DISC Model of Human Behavior over the last decade, though, I've learned that this is only one variation of the truth behind building great business relationships. Two out of every three people we interact with on any given day will indeed need to like someone—at some level—before they'll begin to trust them. Those *people-oriented* folks place a high priority on enjoyable interaction. If there's no personal connection, they may never reach a point where they can build trust.

That said, the remaining one-third of us who are more *task-oriented* will generally need to trust someone before they'll ever begin to like them. When I first learned about this simple yet profound difference, it was as if the heavens had opened! Previously, the folks who appeared to automatically like and trust everyone struck me as naïve. And I'm sure those same folks saw my lack of interest in being friends with anyone I didn't trust as just plain cold. While this is a subtle variation, it still plays a crucial role in how displaying company values affects relationships.

As a *task-oriented* client or customer, we would likely not move forward with a transaction if we see the person we're dealing with as not aligning with their company's values—or our own values, for that matter. Even in a longstanding business relationship, a mismatch between values and behavior can destroy trust right away. *People-oriented* customers and clients may maintain some trust for a bit longer, but seeing the disconnect between actions and values harms their relationship with the person they deal with directly, which will eventually burn the bridge. (Remember the thousand bridges from before?)

While the timing may vary slightly, failing to uphold a business's core values will impact the relationships with its customers. But it won't stop there. Although not all members of the surrounding community may be existing customers, how members of an organization exemplify the stated core values will undoubtedly be something they all pay attention to. Regardless of their people or task focus in the equation, few will ever line up to be new clients without being able to like *and* trust the organization—or the people it's comprised of.

However, standing firm on our core values and consistently working to serve the people who depend on us can earn passionate support that exceeds even the best marketing initiatives.

Strong Values Earn Passionate Support

Someone at any level of an organization can damage relationships with long-term clients and the community around them through behavior inconsistent with their core values. Regardless of whether their primary focus is on the people involved or the task at hand, clients and community members will like us less, and lose our trust, if our behaviors do not align with what we profess as our core values. Yet the inverse holds equally true.

I once heard Marcus Buckingham explain how we approach companies differently when we *like* them compared to when we *love* them. Buckingham said that while we do business with companies we *like*, we go out of our way to tell the world about a company (or product) we *love*. And telling the world about a company certainly isn't exclusive to the ones we *love*. If anything, being alienated by a company—or even someone representing that company—incites every bit as much word of mouth. Think about it: how often have you taken the time to give anyone a three-star review on Amazon or Google? The one-star reviews nearly always share why the customer was dissatisfied. For the four or five-star reviews to include that same level of detail, there was something about the experience the customer truly *loved*.

> **While we do business with companies we *like*, we go out of our way to tell the world about a company (or product) we *love*.**

Before we delve into specific steps for incorporating our values into the experience we provide our clients, as well as the communities we serve (or even the measurable ways doing so will benefit our company) let's consider it from the highest and most general sense. Just as our team members rally around strong values they've seen us model, the same thing happens with clients and community members who see us stand for things they believe matter. Unfortunately, most folks don't get to see anything like that very frequently. Think back to John Maxwell's comment I referenced before about only five percent of anyone we interact with working to exceed what's expected of them. Since I'm convinced his estimate is a bit high, being willing to uphold a core set of company values will undoubtedly go a long way toward ensuring we exceed what our clients and the communities we're a part of expect from us. When we're willing to do that routinely, they may find a reason to *love* us rather than just *like* us. And that's where our strong values can build passionate support from those who know us best.

Earning this type of support doesn't come easy, and it won't happen quickly. In many cases, it may not seem worth it. Moving forward, we'll work through why it's worth pushing forward even when it's tough.

Can You Build a Great Reach Without Values?

Having referenced my last experience attempting to find some type of sustenance from the building beside those large golden arches, I'll challenge you to think back a few decades to what you could expect. When I was a kid, it was such a treat! For years, there was only one location in our area—and that didn't even have a playground. The kids' meals came with great toys, and the milkshake machine was always in working order. We lived about thirty miles out of town, so any visit was a special occasion. Oh, how times have changed...

Fast-forward to today. I can list at least a dozen locations within a half hour of me where I could order the same thing I did as a kid, but what I'd get in the bag would be a far cry from what it was all those years ago—and we all know the milkshake machine will be broken! With all this in mind, that company still has incredible visibility worldwide. However, I can't say that what they're known for lines up with their values.

Now think about where you go for God's chicken sandwich. The number of locations throughout the Shenandoah Valley is similar to what I remember of those prestigious arches some forty years ago. Still, you'd agree that what we can all expect when we visit one is a wildly different level of service (and quality) than what we could ever hope to get anywhere near those arches today. Since our son had two years of hands-on experience making God's chicken sandwiches while finishing up high school, I had the opportunity to get a glimpse many folks likely haven't had. At the owner and operator level, as well as at the corporate level, that organization does more than ensure a drive-through runs smoothly. Their core values aren't just printed in a manual or on a website; they've instilled those values into the conduct expected of each team member while serving every customer.

> **They've instilled those values into the conduct
> expected of each team member
> while serving every customer.**

While I can't make a comparison using current prices, I don't recall the two companies ever being very close. Still, the drive-through line can frequently wrap around one of them at any time of day, while you'd rarely be three cars back at the other. Even then, the line will likely move all the way around the former before the third car gets the *wrong* food at the latter.

Both companies have a vast reach. In fact, the arches are one of the most recognized brands globally. But what you and I have come to expect today is significantly different from each of those companies. Although they're not directly competing with one another on price, both operate in the same general space. Based on my experience with each over the last decade, how those organizations have built their core values into performance at all levels directly impacts their reach—both positively and negatively.

A great marketing campaign can undoubtedly increase the number of people who know a company's name, but how the people in that company embody its core values will play a critical role in determining whether those people are excited to do business there.

With that in mind, let's look at some of the consequences of violating our business's core values.

Not Just Broken Milkshake Machines...

While I was intentional about not mentioning either organization's name previously, I don't doubt that you had an obvious picture of the one with broken milkshake machines and the one serving God's chicken sandwich. And you certainly weren't alone! A cxtoday.com article called "McDonald's Is Failing on Customer Satisfaction, Report Finds[19]" opens with this:

> A customer satisfaction report has found that burger behemoth McDonald's is the poorest-performing major restaurant in the US.

Conducted by the American Customer Satisfaction Index organization (ACSI), McDonald's received the lowest ACSI rating across all full-service and fast-food restaurants.

At the other end of the scale, Chick-fil-A claimed the top spot for the 10th consecutive year, strengthening its position as the King of fast-food customer satisfaction.

> **A customer satisfaction report has found that burger behemoth McDonald's is the poorest-performing major restaurant in the US.**

I cited an article called "The Poetry of Purpose: Inspirational Purpose Statement Examples[20]" in *Leading With A Clear Purpose* that used McDonald's mission, purpose, and values statements as an example of how far companies can vary from each. The article listed these as the core values holding up those golden arches: *serve, inclusion, integrity, community,* & *family.*

Serve, the first listed, was defined as "we put our guests and people first." I'll ask you, if that value was being modeled by leadership—even remotely—throughout the organization, is it likely that they'd be receiving "the lowest ratings across all full-service and fast-food restaurants"? It seems like that may be more than even the most reliable milkshake machine could fix...

Truth be told, I only bring up the milkshake machines because it's become a running joke. For any joke to resonate, though, there needs to be at least some validity to it. And just like most of us have been denied ice cream or a milkshake, it's clear that many others have had similar experiences where the folks behind the counter did not put the guests first. It's also clear that what I observed while our son learned all about those amazing chicken sandwiches wasn't exclusive to our local stores.

The moral of this part of the story is that you and I have both made decisions, as consumers, about which organizations we're willing to do business with regularly. Those decisions typically tie directly back to whether the leaders in these companies choose to model their organizational values and how they've set clear expectations for their teams to do the same. From time to time, we see raging boycotts that make headlines because a company has alienated some of its customers. More frequently, though, we vote silently with our money and opt to do business with those who have demonstrated values that align with our own.

I'm not suggesting that it will ever be a cakewalk for any leader to model the core values defined for their business consistently. It's just as challenging to set high expectations on how their team members exemplify those values and to maintain accountability when someone falls short. That said, failing to do either kills profitability in many areas of that business—and I detailed these two issues in back-to-back chapters of *What's KILLING YOUR Profitability? (It ALL Boils Down to Leadership!)*. Building the foundation of our organization on values consistently will always require making hard decisions.

Taking the "West Point" Approach

While we may be able to allocate sufficient marketing dollars to ensure our brand has an extended reach, the consequences of not consistently modeling our core organizational values— for our team and everyone we hope to reach—won't stop at dealing with broken milkshake machines. Leaders who fail to provide a strong example will not only struggle to rally their team around the values outlined in the handbook, but, sooner or later, they'll also impact the way clients interact with the business. As leaders, though, we can avoid all of that. But that choice will not be the path of least resistance.

My first direct interaction with a man who has made a tremendous impact on my life over the past 25+ years was in January 1999. I had heard tales of a character named Terry Ward for several months before that, but I had never met him personally. Terry covered two of the sixteen hours involved with the initial behavior-based safety training I was squirming through. The content he shared taught me a great deal about human behavior, but his delivery left an even bigger impression. Being new to the Shenandoah Valley (from Massachusetts) and having recently left the United States Army, his approach was different than anyone I had encountered to that point in my life. If someone yawned, which is nearly impossible to avoid when putting a dozen press operators in a training room for two straight days, he'd throw a candy bar at them. He was nothing short of intense, and I had no idea at the time how much he'd sow into my life over the following years.

Terry's topic during those two hours was the role consequences have in how each of us chooses our behaviors. Rather than attempting to cover all that here, I'll stick with the part that still resonates with me today. Terry rarely talks about himself; he's incredibly humble. However, through a brief story shared during that session, he revealed what was instilled in him during his time at the United States Military Academy. He said that one of the primary tenets drilled into him was the importance of consistently choosing the harder right over the easier wrong. He went on to explain that choosing a safe behavior would always be harder, requiring at least as much time as performing a task in a way that created more risk. He's rarely mentioned his West Point experience since, but that single reference was enough.

> **One of the primary tenets drilled into him was the importance of consistently choosing the harder right over the easier wrong.**

As leaders, we'll have the same choice regarding how we model (or don't model) the core values of our organization. On any given day, it will be far easier to skirt the edges or justify how our choices are good enough. Eventually, though, failing to choose the harder right will permeate the team around, impacting the clients we should be serving at the highest level possible as well as our community. From there, it's only a matter of time before going with the easier wrong takes a toll on our company's reputation as well as our bottom-line results.

We'll look at that more soon. Before that, though, we need to work through some simple steps we can each take to exemplify our values for our clients and community.

Rallying Your Community Around Your Values

As I mentioned before, a lot of people being familiar with your company's name and building a great reach that makes a positive impact on everyone around you are two very different things. Whether you prefer God's chicken sandwich or two all-beef patties (although I'm not so sure about the beef part anymore) with special sauce, lettuce, and cheese on a sesame seed bun, both organizations are well-known. However, how the masses perceive them at this point is deeply tied to the steps leaders, both corporately and locally, have taken to model each business's core values—and to hold team members accountable for living out those same values.

The reality is that you and I, as clients of an organization or just living in the communities where they operate, do care about how they exemplify their values. And that feeling is not exclusive to large organizations. If anything, it matters even more for those of us working in and running small businesses. When we take this to heart and consistently choose the harder right over the easier wrong, we can begin to rally an entire community around the core values we're working to model for our teams!

> **When we take this to heart and consistently choose the harder right over the easier wrong, we can begin to rally an entire community around the core values.**

While McDonald's and Chick-fil-A certainly aren't small businesses today, they both started that way, as any company does. And while I wasn't there to watch either, I'd bet that Ray Kroc and Truett Cathy were incredibly diligent in how they worked each day to model the values they held most dear. I'd also bet that their personal values were completely aligned with what they founded their respective businesses on. Like many other small businesses starting out, I'd guess that each of them had plenty of opportunities to take shortcuts to capture more profit at any given moment. Had they done that routinely, though, I doubt we'd know the names of their organizations today.

For you and me, the same thing is necessary. To have any hope of rallying our community around the values we've chosen as the foundation for our businesses, we must walk the talk day in and day out. Truth be told, we'll need to develop that habit long before the community as a whole even notices. When we do that long enough, our teams will eventually follow suit; it took Truett Cathy ten years to get his folks to switch from "You're Welcome" to "My Pleasure." As our teams align on those values, some of our most loyal customers or clients may begin to notice. But until then, it's our responsibility as leaders to do whatever we can to recognize the behaviors our team members exhibit in living out our values, and to celebrate even the smallest resultant victories.

This won't be simple early on. In fact, we can expect times when even we struggle to see the difference that solidifying the foundation of our organization around those values is making. Nearly ten years ago, John Maxwell told me and Cindy that no one can expect to be great the first time they do something. Building our values into what our clients and community see from us is no different. To push through when we barely see any progress, we'll need to be intentional about recognizing where we are and reflecting on where we've come from.

Sustaining the Harder Right Requires Reflection

I opened *Leading With A Clear Purpose* with a story detailing the conversation I had with a lifelong friend who shared how one of his businesses no longer provided him with fulfillment while his other, albeit much more physically demanding, kept his heart full all the time. The business that filled his need for purpose was a small (at the time) mixed martial arts gym, where he held classes for all age groups. In a follow-up to that initial discussion, he shared how some of his students get discouraged when they don't feel like they're progressing as quickly as they had hoped.

Since he's the owner and lead coach for everyone there, I challenged him to look for ways he could help them see just how much they've improved, whether that's routinely in one-on-one conversations or by recognizing specific achievements as they occur. Each student faces a really challenging process. Since everyone they're training with is also improving, it can be tough for any of them to see their own progress. And that can quickly become demoralizing, especially for the new guy who rarely comes out on top when going head-to-head.

As important as it is for my friend to be able to highlight the progress each of his students has made, we all share a similar need: as members of a team and as leaders of that team. The work we'll need to do to rally a community around our organization's core values will seem futile at times. As I've already suggested a few times, we'll frequently be faced with the option of moving toward the easier wrong instead of sticking to the harder right that aligns with our values. When we're under constant pressure to achieve bottom-line results, sticking to our values over the long haul can seem like we're not gaining any ground at all.

> **When we're under constant pressure to achieve bottom-line results, sticking to our values over the long haul can seem like we're not gaining any ground at all.**

For those of us who have accepted the responsibility of leadership, especially when we're *fast-paced* and *task-oriented* with measurable results serving as a primary driving force, slowing down enough to reflect on how much we've accomplished rarely happens. Most leaders I've known over the years tend to keep their heads down and push through anything and everything that comes their way. That constant focus on getting things done doesn't typically allow for much reflection on where they've come from. Now, I'm not throwing stones at anyone guilty of this! Without Cindy building time into our schedule for this type of reflection, I don't think I'd have done it on my own. And I doubt I could have kept focused on our clear purpose without her taking this step.

In 2012/2013, just as we were finally getting our heads above water financially after a near-foreclosure thanks to a fiasco with Wells Fargo, we found ourselves in a scenario where we had no choice but to address a situation with some business associates that went against our values. We took a stand, but that stand came with substantial financial consequences (to the tune of six figures in lost revenue annually since). As tough as that was at the time, both for our bank account and because we quickly learned that some of the folks we had considered close friends were not, we've never regretted that decision; and, in the ten-plus years since, we've had several more occasions that forced us to make similar ones. Each time, we've chosen to stick with the values we hold most dear. And each time, it's definitely been *harder*—financially and physically, and often even emotionally.

At any point along the way, it would have been very easy to look at where we were right then and throw in the proverbial towel. We've always had a busy schedule, but that's grown exponentially with all that's involved in starting and running our business. Without Cindy being so intentional about us dedicating time to reflect on our overall progress as well as the successes we've had along the way, we may not have sustained those values. Without that, we wouldn't have had a solid foundation around which to rally a community, or even have a shot at being viewed as an overnight success.

Momentum Builds Into an "Overnight Success"

If Cindy and I had only been measuring our accomplishments by reviewing our bank statements and retirement account balances, making some of the decisions we've been faced with over the last fifteen years would have been substantially harder. Reflecting on even the most minor personal or business victories, though, has been critical in helping us sustain the harder right to live out our values daily—despite varying levels of nonsense on any given day.

> **Reflecting on even the most minor personal or business victories, though, has been critical in helping us sustain the harder right to live out our values daily.**

I remember sitting in a group of a few hundred people at the end of the event that completed my initial licensing to use John Maxwell's material. During that session, one of the speakers emphasized the importance of having additional products or services to offer our clients. I understood that concept from a bricks-and-mortar aspect, but I was so new to the idea of operating my own business that I couldn't picture how it could ever happen for me.

Not long after that, I started a weekly email series, now branded as *A Daily Dose of Leadership*, which reaches tens of thousands of people each month through emails and subsequent blog posts. In early 2018, Cindy and I shared our *Emerging Leader Development* course (as a specific package) for the very first time. While presenting those lessons, we decided to offer participants who complete the course ongoing support for their leadership journey. This has since grown into our *Leading At The Next Level* program, which features more than 150 hours of material that we've created. As I write this, our website averages over 200,000 visitors per month. We've contributed to two collaborative books, written and published the Amazon #1 best-sellers *What's KILLING Your Profitability?* and *Leading With A Clear Purpose*, and recently hosted an event for leaders from over 125 organizations in the region. As I sat with those few hundred people I had never met in August 2015, I wouldn't have believed any of this was possible.

Just as clearly as I remember that feeling as I heard that suggestion to have additional products or services to offer, I remember the manufacturing plant manager I was working for a year before telling me that I was making the biggest mistake of my career by leaving the company for whom I had then worked my entire adult life. Please know that I don't share any of the things we've accomplished to boast. Quite honestly, we've worked harder (and longer hours) since starting our business than we ever had previously—and we have always worked pretty damn hard! I share it because none of this would have happened without ferociously standing by our personal core values and routinely reflecting on just the smallest bits of progress along the way.

Before wrapping up this part, I need to clarify why I referenced our *personal* core values rather than the core values of our *business*. Anything we've accomplished to this point, as well as any success we achieve moving forward in our business, is based on a foundation of the values we hold personally. We don't have the luxury of separating our personal feelings from how we operate our business. And I've never seen anyone lead effectively over the long haul when they try to do so. One of the reasons for the positive experiences I know you can picture when I mention the service at Chick-fil-A is that the Cathy family modeled strong values in their personal lives and the business, setting high expectations for the owners of each location to do the same. Having worked closely with my friend, Craig, for several years now, I know he ran a company with nearly a billion in annual revenue, just as he runs the four small businesses he and his wife own today, all on a foundation of their core *personal* values.

Whether we're leading a small team, operating our own business, or running a large organization, modeling our core values—especially when it's hard—will provide our teams with something they'll happily rally around. Doing that consistently, over time, will provide our clients and the community around us with plenty of reasons to do the same. Eventually, living by those core values will build a reputation for our organizations that impacts everything we're working to achieve, and that's what we'll work through next!

CHAPTER SIX

WHO ULTIMATELY CARES ABOUT YOUR VALUES? (IT'S JUST YOUR REPUTATION...)

As heavy as the weight can often be in any leadership role, we must not lose sight of exactly who, ultimately, cares about the core values of our organization: everyone. How we're known, up close and from a distance, all boils down to whether we've been willing to build those values into the foundation of everything we do—and, in turn, everything each member of our team does. While the reputation we become known for, such as running a smooth drive-through or the milkshake machines always being broken, often reaches more people than we ever serve directly, it all starts with the clients and community we serve, which begins with how we've rallied our teams around those values.

When we looked at what can happen when that foundation isn't as strong as we need it to be, I shared something I found in a Forbes.com article called "Rethinking the Value of Core Values[21]" by Curt Steinhorst saying,

> "Core values have weight, especially when they're *truthful* and *focused on what matters to the community* within the organization. If they're hollow, corrupted, misguided, or pretentious, they carry with them a falsehood that can trap and divide an organization. But if they are drawn from and representative of the community they serve, they can have the strength of steel. Like any principle or strategy, core values are difficult to forge and take time to develop and cure; but once they're well-formed, they sustain you through everything else."

While the broken milkshake machines certainly don't have anywhere near the negative impact as the Enron scandal that I detailed after sharing this statement previously, you can still picture the restaurant chain's sign each time I joke about it. If your experience is even close to what mine has been over the last ten years, you have come to a similar conclusion: the only way what I order will make it into *my* bag is if I put it there myself... I mean, seriously, does anyone really leave one of their locations thinking, "I'm lovin' it!"?

However wide our reach may be—whether global, nationwide, or local—the reputation that precedes us stems from the culture our organization operates within. And that culture is based on the values that we, along with the leaders on our teams, have modeled for everyone within the company who looks to us for leadership. Our decisions to consistently exemplify what we've defined as our core values or to justify behavior that doesn't align with those values may seem insignificant on any given day, but this always has a cascading effect. Over time, for good or for bad, even our smallest decisions—whether to uphold or contradict our values—permeate our culture and shape the reputation our entire organization is known for. Make no mistake, our reputation has a direct impact on our overall results. We'll look at that soon enough. First, though, we need to consider what we want to be known for versus what we're known for.

What ARE You Known For?

An article called "Workplace culture and its impact on corporate reputation[22]" from a UK-based group Igniyte, an organization dedicated to managing corporate reputations, opened with this:

> A company's reputation is all about how other people view the brand. Their perception derives from several factors, including media coverage, the CEO's social media sites, customer reviews, and whether there is a healthy workplace culture internally. What employees think about the company's culture and workplace culture is hugely important when it comes to its external reputation.

> **What employees think about the company's culture
> and workplace culture is hugely important
> when it comes to its external reputation.**

With that in mind, I'll stress this once more: our team members, our clients, and the community we operate in directly all care about our values, but so does everyone else who ever hears anything about us!

But hold on, Wes—how did we go from the simple behaviors we use internally to model our values to something as far-reaching as how people view our overall brand? The folks at Igniyte went on to share this, connecting the dots between reputation, culture, and values—and tying all of them to an organization's results:

> Company culture is a catch-all term for its set of behaviors, values, and belief systems that dictate how it operates both externally and internally. A strong culture in the workplace is vital for enhancing employee engagement and overall organizational success.
>
> Workplace culture, then, impacts and influences the following:
>
> 1. How customers perceive the organization's culture (its external reputation).
>
> 2. How employee engagement manifests.
>
> 3. How all stakeholders view and interact with the company/brand.
>
> From this, we can extrapolate that a healthy workplace culture that accurately reflects and lives the company's core values boosts employee happiness, its reputation, and organizational success.

> **A strong culture in the workplace is vital
> for enhancing employee engagement
> and overall organizational success.**

Later, we'll dig into how our reputation influences the results we achieve. First, though, we need to be honest with ourselves about whether our reputation is what we want it to be. It's one thing for our values to be listed online, or for the boss to mention them in a soapbox rant, but that doesn't mean anyone has connected with or lives by those values. As a reminder of how often this happens, think back to the article I referenced before from MIT Sloan Management Review called "When It Comes to Culture, Does Your Company Walk the Talk?[23]" saying, "We found that more than 80% published an official set of corporate values on their website" and "more than three-quarters of CEOs interviewed in a major business magazine discussed their company's culture or core values — even when not specifically asked about it." That same article closed by emphasizing, "Unfortunately, many organizations' core values are so generic that they could easily serve as fodder for a *Dilbert* cartoon."

So what about that honest, clear-eyed look? What should we be asking ourselves? Several years ago, Cindy and I were part of a small group on a call with Mark Cole and Jeff Henderson (who had just written *Know What You're FOR* at the time), where Jeff challenged us with these three questions:

- What *do you want to be* known for?
- What *are* you known for?
- Do they match?

At first glance, these questions appear to be focused solely on our personal or organizational reputation; however, our response to the third ties back to our company culture and how we, as leaders in that company, have (or have not) worked to model what we have listed as our core values on a routine basis. Think about it: do they really "put guests and people first" when the milkshake machines are broken company-wide? Our reputation, the culture it's built on, and the values that drive that culture are based far more on what people see than what we say.

What They See IS What They Get

So, who ultimately cares about the core values we model, both personally and in our organizations? Everyone does! The reputation of our company is indeed built on the values we consistently exemplify. For far too many individuals and businesses, the answer to that third question Jeff Henderson challenged us with is an unfortunate *NO*.

Companies nearly always (around 80% of the time based on the stats I just referenced again) *say* what they want to be known for by posting their values with wonderfully crafted definitions on their websites for the world to see, and then the executives pontificate about those values to anyone pointing a camera or microphone in their direction—whether that same message ever gets to the rest of their teams or not.

How often have you heard someone say, "What you see is what you get!" detailing their aim to be genuine in all that they do? Hearing that statement isn't uncommon. The validity of it, though, depends on the source. Just as posting meticulous core values on a website or reciting them in an interview, talking is the easy part. We can detail what we want to be known for, but what we're actually known for—internally with our team members, externally with our clients, and even more broadly through the reputation we build over time—ties right back to "What you see is what you get!"

If what we want to be known for doesn't align with what we are known for, we must examine any possible reasons we can identify that may be driving this discrepancy. Perhaps we haven't been as straightforward as we'd hoped in conveying what our values truly mean; am I the only one who has ever thought I explained something in detail, only to find out later that I completely missed the mark? I know it's hard to believe, but I've done it more than a few times—just ask Cindy! Or maybe we shared the perfect message once, saw our folks connect the dots as they heard it, then neglected ever to follow up to solidify just how important those values are every single day. Had Truett Cathy said "My Pleasure" just one time, rather than for ten whole years, we may have never even learned about the amazingness of God's chicken sandwich... But maybe, just maybe, what we say in detailing those values isn't lining up with what people see in our actions.

> **Maybe, just maybe, what we say in detailing those values isn't lining up with what people see in our actions.**

Whether it's from a misunderstanding, a difference in perception, a lack of consistency in sharing the message, or we've completely dropped the ball in living out the values we want to be known for, what people *see* is far more important than anything we ever *say*. We can count on the people closest to us to duplicate the example we provide. What our teams do routinely will have an immediate impact on the clients we serve and the community in which we operate. And eventually, even if we're blessed with a longstanding history where the milkshake machines were once dependable, what people *see* will overtake what we *say* and anything we've said or done leading up to that point. That will become our reputation—and that reputation will impact our results.

A Reputation That Drives Results

I'll ask you one more time: *Who ultimately cares about your values?* Our immediate team members most certainly do. And so do the clients we serve directly, as well as the community we're a part of. But everyone else who hears about us will, too, and all of that will impact the results we achieve in one way or another.

I often reference the eighteen-month period during which I hired 225 people, resulting in a net headcount increase of less than thirty. The work performed in any given area within that facility hadn't changed; it was always fast-paced and physically demanding. If anything, working conditions had improved somewhat over time as technology advanced. And even though there was a ton of mandatory overtime, that had been the case since the company started operating locally in 1961. The most significant change I saw in the final few years I worked in that organization was the interaction between the local management team and the rest of the workforce. Over the course of a decade or so, many of the longest-tenured management team members had retired, left the company for other opportunities, or taken on new roles elsewhere within the organization. While most of the changes occurred one at a time, there were several key changes within just a few months, about two years before I decided to move on. Interestingly enough, those key changes occurred just before the most significant increase in turnover I had seen in the nearly two decades with the company. I can't say it was a coincidence, either...

In chapter nine of *The 21 Irrefutable Laws of Leadership*[24], John Maxwell defines "The Law of Magnetism" by saying, "Who you attract is not determined by what you *want*. It's determined by who you *are*." One of the new management team members who started in that short period served as the engineering manager. He was new to the area and, arguably, looking to use any success he could take credit for at that location as a stepping stone for more prestigious roles within the company or elsewhere. He wasted no time in alienating nearly everyone he interacted with on the shop floor, but he didn't need anything from them since he already knew more than everyone who had been working there longer than he had been alive. Since he only dealt with the production employees in passing, that had a limited impact on their results. With his direct team, though, it was a different story.

> **"Who you attract is not determined by what you *want*. It's determined by who you *are*."**

The most senior salaried engineers tolerated him, mainly because most of them excelled in their roles; he was more of an annoyance to work around. The hourly team members under his thumb had far less leeway. These highly skilled maintenance mechanics and diemakers were indeed critical to keeping the operation running, so dependability had always been a core value embraced by the engineering team. Under his iron fist, though, any discretionary time away from work was eliminated—regardless of the reason it was needed. The majority of the hourly team members had perfect attendance most of the time, and one of them maintained that for 35 consecutive years. Much of that waned during his tenure; be it a foot of snow, an ice storm, or a family emergency, nothing was excused.

The strict enforcement wasn't a big deal. The attendance policy hadn't changed. What had changed was the example those team members saw him setting. On his best days, he would show up at 8 am and leave around 5 pm, and that was only Monday through Friday. If there was so much moderate rain, you could count on him arriving late or leaving early, possibly both. And there was little chance of catching him in the building between 11:30a and 1:30p; he wasn't about to abide by the twenty minutes he expected his minions to scarf their lunch down in. You can imagine how it affected their feelings about him, this discrepancy between his modeled values and what the highly-skilled team had always held dear. Think back to that Harvard Business Review article I've referenced here, throughout *What's KILLING Your Profitability?* and a few times in *Leading With A Clear Purpose*... Do you think he earned anywhere close to that 57% increase in discretionary effort?

While that's one specific example of how the values modeled (or, in this case, not modeled) by someone in a leadership role impact results—and this example is limited to the hourly team members in his department at that time—the impact most definitely did not stop with his team. Nor was he the only new management team member walking a far different walk than what was expected by the rank-and-file who made up the rest of the workforce. This had an (almost) immediate impact on overall performance. Soon, it spilled over into our ability to recruit quality candidates for the numerous open positions resulting from it.

Eventually, those management changes, and how they exemplified —or failed to exemplify—the values that had been strongly held within that facility for decades impacted what customers around the country experienced from that location. The change was substantial, but it didn't happen overnight.

Perpetuating the Cycle

Prior to my start at the manufacturing facility in early 1996, and for the first fifteen years I worked there, one of the largest and most reliable sources for identifying new candidates was through referrals from respected employees. As you can likely imagine, the referrals from the best employees dried up, with several new managers on staff, mirroring the behavior of the engineering manager I just described. The individuals who had previously been some of the most trusted referral sources no longer wanted to bring anyone they cared about into that atmosphere, and the individuals who were still willing to refer others weren't necessarily those with outstanding credibility.

The Law of Magnetism was working double time! A management team made up primarily of individuals with no real ties to the area and unwilling to develop connections with the workforce, looking more at how they could position themselves for the next rung on their career ladder, was attracting far more candidates who were only interested in immediate compensation rather than folks who wanted to be part of a historically reputable culture.

Through the time I left the organization in late 2014, order fill (the percentage of orders shipped to customers from each business unit) was one of the primary metrics discussed in daily production meetings. If that number fell below 95% in any business unit, it was considered an all-hands-on-deck emergency—and rightfully so! Any business that fails to meet customer demands effectively is at risk of joining its competitors' marketing teams. In speaking with friends who are still with that company several years later, I learned it had become common for the order fill rate to be as low as 75% on any given day.

How that handful of new managers modeled their own core values, rather than aligning with the values the workforce had rallied around for years leading up to that, quickly impacted their direct reports' willingness to go above and beyond the call of duty—and in some cases, just to meet standard expectations. The lack of quality candidates being referred by our most trusted team members soon made staffing a much more challenging process. Over time, the reputation that the management team became known for in the community resulted in the company being a place where people applied when they couldn't get a job anywhere else, despite its continued offering of one of the best overall compensation packages in the area.

The challenges in recruiting and the decline in discretionary effort, resulting in such low order fill rates, contributed to the loss of several large accounts and negatively impacted the company's perception on Wall Street. None of this occurred immediately, but each piece impacted the others, perpetuating the cycle. How we, as leaders in our respective organizations, model the values that matter the most to us will gradually show up throughout our teams, soon after for the customers we serve, and eventually for everyone else who knows anything about us—regardless of the message we share in our commercials or on social media.

> **How we, as leaders in our respective organizations, model the values that matter the most to us will gradually show up throughout our teams, soon after for the customers we serve, and eventually for everyone else who knows anything about us.**

While I've profiled a company with a once-strong reputation that spiraled downward when a group of new managers chose not to exemplify its longstanding, foundational values, the inverse has just as much potential for impacting results. Either way, whether we live out our core company values each day or preach one thing while doing another, our reputations will eventually reflect our behavior. As leaders, we must be intentional about walking the talk, recognizing others who do the same, and addressing issues that don't align with our values—and doing all of this consistently.

A Clear-Eyed Look

During a conversation Cindy and I had with Carly Fiorina several years ago, she emphasized the importance of taking a "clear-eyed look at our existing state" if we wanted to have any hope of achieving our desired future state—personally, professionally, and with the entire team we're leading. The engineering manager I mentioned earlier seemed to believe he was exceptional, as did several of his peers who were even newer to the management team than he was.

That kind of arrogance didn't sit well with anyone he dealt with, especially those who reported to him. The engineering, maintenance, and tool & die shop had fewer employees than any of the production areas. Still, the service those folks provided was imperative to maintaining workflow throughout the facility. While it didn't align with the core values that served as a foundation for the reputation the company had built locally over the decades leading up to that point, his behavior (and the behavior of several others serving on the management team with him) made it obvious to everyone around exactly what he did value: himself.

The longer this went on, and the more people were impacted by the behaviors of such managers, the more it influenced the results we were able to achieve, the quality of candidates we could attract, and what the company was now known for in the area; the cycle was definitely perpetuating!

If we genuinely want our core values to serve as a solid foundation for what our team is built on, for our clients and community to rally around, and for our reputation to be known far and wide, the clear-eyed look at our current state that Carly emphasized is something we need to do consistently. Regardless of how much we strive to model the values we hold up for everyone to see, there will inevitably be times when we fall short of the mark.

The engineering manager I've referenced here certainly wasn't the first person to join the local management team from outside the area. Terry Ward (who taught me the importance of choosing the harder right over the easier wrong) was in a very similar situation fifteen years prior. He rubbed some folks the wrong way at times, too. Still, he was very intentional about doing all he possibly could to build relationships, earn respect, and buy-in, and he routinely sought input from folks with more or different experiences. Terry was very aware of how he exemplified the values of the organization he was a part of, and he was willing to take responsibility if he fell short in any way.

Terry didn't earn respect overnight, and the fellow who filled the engineering manager role more than a decade later didn't alienate everyone overnight. In each case, the relationships they had with their immediate teams, as well as others they interacted with throughout that facility, were cultivated over time—for good or for bad—and were a direct reflection of the values they each modeled. The reputations our entire organizations are known for grow stronger or crumble the same way. When, not *if*, we give someone even the perception of not being aligned with our values, it's critical that we own it and do all we can to make it right. If one of our team members isn't living up to our core values, we need to address this issue with them and with anyone who may have been impacted.

> **The relationships they had with their immediate teams, as well as others they interacted with throughout that facility, were cultivated over time— for good or for bad—and were a direct reflection of the values they each modeled.**

A few years ago, Mark Cole told me that he "trusts someone who makes mistakes but not someone who makes excuses." We also need to be just as intentional about acknowledging when our team members go above and beyond to model our values; that's what helps solidify a good reputation, and recognized behavior gets repeated.

As we undertake all this, we'll also need to be very clear in explaining exactly why, for our team members, our clients, the local community, and every one our reputation reaches. We can't count on anyone else to tell our story or explain why our values are so vital to us the way we want them told.

Modeling Our Values, and Explaining Why

Even when we've done everything in our power to model the core values our business is built on, we can't just assume that everyone who cares about those values will automatically connect our behaviors to the reputation we're working to establish (or maintain). It's up to us to explain why we've chosen our specific approach. As nice as it would be if everyone understood it all, they're likely consumed with their own issues and have little time left over for anything we may hope they're paying attention to. I've often heard that most people don't want to hear about our problems, and those who do are happy we have them! When it comes to taking the time to think about how any service we provide to our clients exemplifies our core company values, you can bet that clients are far more interested in how we're helping solve their problems than in why we're providing that service in a certain way.

During a recent conversation with a client (who is also a very close friend), I suggested they be very intentional in ensuring that the people in each of the companies they work with are routinely aware of a specific need they have within their given firm. While this client's company is already one of the best in their field, adding that extra bit of talent would help them provide all their clients with more and better service; mentioning this need would in no way be perceived as a lack of capability for what they currently offer.

My friend's response was: "As frequently as we work with each of those other companies, I would think they'd naturally point someone with that skill set in my direction…"

While I understood why they felt this way, I shared how many times someone Cindy and I had an existing business relationship with solicited support from another business simply because they had no idea we offered what they needed—and we could have easily delivered exponentially more return on their investment since we already know a lot about their team. In most cases, these clients (ours and my friend's) are so busy keeping their own plates spinning that we're just not at the top of their minds. This isn't necessarily because they don't care about the relationship we have with them; our needs, or how and why we're working to model our core values, aren't the first thing they think about. If we're not intentional about staying on their radar, can we really blame them?

If we want the values we hold most dear to be a solid part of the reputation we're known for far and wide, we cannot leave any of that to chance. Not only will we need to discuss those values consistently, but we'll also need to connect everything we do as an organization to those values and provide detailed explanations for our approach.

All too often, individuals and organizations alike shy away from this out of concern that it will come across as self-serving or manipulative.

> **Not only will we need to discuss those values consistently, but we'll also need to connect everything we do as an organization to those values and provide detailed explanations for our approach.**

As I mentioned earlier, when explaining the importance of defining exactly what our values mean, the only individuals I've ever known to do this in a manipulative way were also manipulative in everything else they did. The best example I've ever heard was very intentional about making sure everyone knew exactly why He did what He did.

A Reputation for Serving, Based on Our Values

There's a massive difference between touting how amazing we are and explaining how or why our actions align with our values. We've all been around folks who have a title that carries some level of authority and seen them pound their chest about how important they are or why everyone around needs to follow all their commands. If that's our underlying objective when discussing our values, you can bet that anyone listening will, sooner or later, see right through it. However, if the explanation we provide is genuine and detailed, explaining why we're willing to do everything in our power to exceed our clients' expectations, it's a whole different ball game.

At this risk of alienating some folks, including a few who may even share my faith, let's consider this from a Christian perspective. I have two close friends who are very open about being atheists. Both are men of principle and some of the most morally sound people I've ever known. Over the decades we've been friends, I've seen numerous people all but attack them for not aligning with a stereotypical Christian worldview. If that were me in their shoes, being scolded over differing views, that would only push me farther away—be that about a particular faith or anything else. Quite honestly, both of the men I'm referring to have demonstrated far more character in the time I've known them than many of the loudest I've ever been around in any denomination.

All said, I've never been apologetic with them about my own faith; I've just never attempted to shove it down their throats. But each time I've been able to serve them in some way, I try to emphasize that I'm doing it not just because they're my friend but also because that's the example Jesus provided in Mark 10:42-45 (NIV)[25]:

> "You know that the rulers in this world lord it over their people, and officials flaunt their authority over those under them. But among you it will be different. Whoever wants to be a leader among you must be your servant, and whoever wants to be first among you must be the slave of everyone else. For even the Son of Man came not to be served but to serve others and to give his life as a ransom for many."

Inserting such reasoning into any conversation, with either of them, allows them to scrutinize every bit of my less-than-perfect behavior. So be it; I'm judged by people I respect less than those two friends every single day... I share that with them because I care about them, not in an attempt to tell them they're wrong and I'm right.

As we explain how our behaviors connect with our values, the same thing holds true. If we can detail why we're willing to go above and beyond in providing our products or services, it's no longer about why we're great, more about why we believe everyone we interact with deserves that level of service. It's similar with the difference between a manager who demands that everyone cater to them and a leader who actively seeks ways to benefit their team members. Modeling our core values should increase the level of service we provide to everyone we interact with. Explaining it just helps connect the dots. All in all, we'll need to ensure consistency at every step.

Modeling our core values should increase the level of service we provide to everyone we interact with.

A Reputation Built on Consistency, Over Time...

To build a reputation that drives results, one that each person who ever hears about us will connect with our core values, being intentional in our approach to providing world-class service is essential. Being clear about why we're willing to do it is part of our responsibility as leaders. But doing any of this on occasion won't get the job done. We'll have to model our values every single day. We'll also need to ensure that everyone on our team understands exactly why we're doing this and how they're expected to do the same. Doing either consistently won't be nearly as simple as printing those values in a handbook, painting them on a wall, or adding them to our website. That's where discipline comes into play, and that kind of discipline is often the key difference between effectively leading a team and just managing the actions of the people reporting to us.

> **That kind of discipline is often the key difference between effectively leading a team and just managing the actions of the people reporting to us.**

All said, this discipline of consistency, especially when we feel like we've beaten the horse to death, can wear out even the most driven executives. Starting off *Leading With A Clear Purpose*, I emphasized the importance of identifying exactly why we accepted the responsibility for leading an organization or just a small team. Without a clear and definite purpose, living out and detailing our values—over and over again—can be a heavy load. Not only will we need our own clear purpose for leading, but we'd do well to connect those values directly to the purpose we're working to achieve as an organization.

> **Without a clear and definite purpose, living out and detailing our values —over and over again—can be a heavy load.**

Our example sets the process in motion, but bringing the team along with us on the journey is how we'll build modeling our values into a culture. This culture yields the reputation our organization is known for far and wide. That's where the second half of *Leading With A Clear Purpose* comes into play: helping our team members identify their own clear purpose and connecting that with our organizational purpose. With that connection made, tying our core values to purpose can give meaning to work that may otherwise lead to burnout—especially when the process takes longer than any of us wants, and we do not see significant results.

There's no way around it; building a great reputation takes time and consistent effort. Whatever reputation we're known for from a distance will be based on the culture we've built within our teams and what the clients and community we support directly experience from us. And, like it or not, that internal culture falls completely on how we've routinely modeled our core values for everyone we lead. Consistency gets the process started, and connecting our values to a clear purpose will help create sustainability, something we'll begin working through soon.

SECTION TWO

PRACTICAL APPLICATIONS FOR BUILDING A VALUES-DRIVEN CULTURE

Ready to make values more than words? Chapters 7–10 deliver practical tools to weave core values into every facet of leadership. From simple daily practices to building a culture of accountability, this section draws on direct experience with clients who transformed their organizations through consistent, values-driven actions. Learn how leaders fostered team buy-in, reduced turnover, and boosted profitability by aligning behaviors with values like integrity and dependability. These chapters show how to create sustainable expectations and a lasting legacy, using real-world examples to inspire action. Following Section One's case for values, this section empowers leaders to apply them effectively, setting the stage for a framework to ensure your organization's values become its defining strength.

CHAPTER SEVEN

LAYING A FOUNDATION ON VALUES: SIMPLE PRACTICES

We began by examining how values serve as the foundation for every organization, and how things can go wrong when that foundation isn't in place. From there, we worked through the importance of clearly defining our organizational values and how doing so can truly rally our team members, earn buy-in from our clients and immediate community, and build the reputation we're known for even more widely. Now it's time to get to work! Let's lay a foundation for the organizations we lead that's based on our core values.

I've recently seen some images on social media of existing and proposed skyscrapers, with the tallest currently being over 2,700' in Dubai and one a complete 500' taller set for a 2028 completion in Saudi Arabia. Over the years, I've heard folks comment on how much goes into creating a foundation that can support (and sustain) a structure of that magnitude. In many cases, laying these foundations can take up to a year. According to the website for Sameer Building Construction[26], the foundation for the Twin Towers of Malaysia is around 400' deep, supporting the nearly 1,500' tall structure. The work involved and the necessary overall depth depend on the soil conditions and the type of materials used. Excavation for these foundations takes a tremendous amount of time. And even after the digging and all the work to prepare for pouring the foundation, the concrete curing process (especially when it's that much involved) is extremely slow. According to Study.com[27], the concrete poured for the Hoover Dam in the 1930s is still curing today.

Now, imagine you're an investor backing a project like this. A year after the ceremonial ground-breaking, you still don't see anything resembling a structure above the privacy fence surrounding the construction area. I can't speak for you, but I know my limited patience would be worn thin if I didn't have a complete understanding of the process and project timeline. As amazingly beautiful as a building of that magnitude can be, the far less attractive part—the foundation— will ultimately determine whether it stands the test of time.

While most of us will never be intricately involved in building a skyscraper, I'd bet we've all had at least some visibility of building a modest home. The scale is significantly smaller, but the process isn't wildly different; the foundation still supports the end product. Our core personal and organizational values serve as the foundation for how we lead our teams. Like the foundation for a skyscraper or a home, much of the work we do to ensure our values are indeed serving as the foundation for our organization will go unnoticed early on—and sustaining that with limited results (or no visible results at all) can be challenging.

Although I've never been involved in a construction project as large as the skyscrapers I've referenced here, my first hands-on experience in the complete building process of a home was more than thirty years ago, and that taught me some valuable lessons about the importance of a solid foundation.

Laying a Foundation is Hard Work!

My first full-time gig in construction started about a month after I turned fifteen. Earlier that spring, my dad asked if I planned to get a car when I was old enough to drive. "Of course I do!" was my immediate response, and he went on to let me know that I'd probably want to consider making some money so I could pay for it.

He connected me with a guy he knew who owned a residential contracting business nearby, and the rest, as they say, is history! His crew was building close to where I lived, so I was able to ride my bicycle to and from work every day for the entire summer. Before getting back to how important a strong foundation is for even a modest home, I want you to picture a fifteen-year-old kid, weighing no more than 130 pounds, carrying a lunchbox and water jug on opposite sides of the handlebars with at least 25 pounds of tools in the nail apron around his waist, riding just a half mile home after trying to keep up with grown men all day in 100-degree heat. Let's call that a life-shaping experience!

Leading up to that summer, I'd helped my dad and his friends with small home improvement projects: vinyl siding, shingle roofs, and some replacement windows. Truthfully, all they allowed me to do was keep the worksite cleaned up, do some basic measuring, and do occasional cutting. Now and then, I climbed onto a roof with them so I could at least feel like I had made a real contribution. All in all, even that limited exposure helped me develop the basic skills necessary to perform adequately in this new full-time (summer) job—but I was most definitely not prepared for the physical demands.

While I had some decent carpentry skills, I wasn't close to being capable of the precision necessary for really any of the finish work. That landed me with the guys starting the projects and doing the framing, and just like those skyscrapers, the start to even a basic home is the foundation. I was quickly trained to operate a shovel while digging footers. No, not a piece of excavating equipment—a shovel like you use to dig holes! I was the guy in the footers, cleaning out the loose dirt left behind by the backhoe. I also became very familiar with a sledgehammer, driving the grade stakes to the appropriate depth for pouring the concrete. I had the privilege of working at the dumb end of the transit, meaning I held the stick, attempting to adjust the height of those stakes without driving them too deep and having to start over.

In the best-case scenario, we were able to complete the inspection and pour the concrete before a heavy thunderstorm passed through. That wasn't always the case, though. On the days we arrived at the job site after a hard rain, the footers that had been dug but not poured were usually filled with water. That water had to be removed before inspection or concrete, so guess who was typically given that task. As you may imagine, a lot of rain on red clay (especially down in those footers) made for a slimy mess. Even in dry conditions, footers are hard work. Add an inch or so of rain to the mix, throw in that red mud for good measure, and you've got yourself a recipe for a downright miserable day!

As difficult as that could be, the worst part of it all was realizing very few people would ever know what went into the process. Similarly, identifying and beginning to model our core business values can seem like it's going unnoticed early on—and maybe even for years. With the possible exception of setting trusses and installing the roof system, laying the foundation for a home is by far the most difficult and physically demanding part of the entire process. Being the first, and often only, person to exemplify the core values we've defined for our company can feel equally demanding! And just like dipping the water out of those footers, feeling like no one sees the work we're putting into living out our values can be hard to overcome.

> ## The worst part of it all was realizing very few people would ever know what went into the process.

A Foundation Gets Little Attention Until There's an Issue

I'd just about bet that unless you were involved in some aspect of the building process or can actually see your home's foundation, you don't know if it consists of 8" cinder blocks, 12" cinder blocks, poured concrete walls, or built directly on a concrete slab. And even if you can answer that, there's far less chance you know how wide the footers were or how many places required a step-up to adjust for grade. To that end, I'd bet most folks know even less about everything that's between their ceiling and the exterior of their roof—be that metal or shingles. Just like all that went into your foundation, the trusses, sheathing, insulation, vapor barrier, and tar paper are all critical to the sustainability of your home—and most people have no earthly idea what each of the things I've listed even are, or why they're essential.

To ensure you're following along, I'll reiterate how much effort goes into each of these. Physically, I don't know if I've ever done harder work than digging and pouring footers, mixing mud for block and brick layers, setting trusses, or putting on shingles or metal roofing. Near the end of my first summer in construction, I tried showing the crew I worked with how tough I was by attempting to carry two bundles of asphalt shingles up an extension ladder to the peak of the roof line. Remember, I weighed around 130 pounds at the time—and each bundle of shingles weighed approximately 70 pounds. Just in case you're not very good at math, those shingles were heavier than I. Just for good measure, add in the 25 pounds or so of tools in the nail bag around my waist, and I'm guessing I was beyond the weight capacity that ladder was rated for. Had the 40-year-old safety and human resource manager version of me been around to see the 15-year-old accident-waiting-to-happen me, who knows what would have transpired!

Do you know when those things I've detailed here come to a homeowner's attention? When there's an issue! Do you have any guesses as to what would likely cause any of those to be on the homeowner's radar? Having water somewhere we don't want it—whether in our basement or crawlspace, or appearing as a wet spot on our ceiling—is the most common reason we learn the intimate details that went into our foundation or roofing system. But regardless of the issue behind this new focus, it's rarely at an ideal time or something we're excited to deal with.

Now, consider the business world; when do core values typically receive the most attention? That's rhetorical. Aside from when executives boast to the media or investors, I can only list a handful of companies (many of which I've referenced throughout this process) that I've seen do more than list their values in a handbook or briefly mention those values in an occasional staff meeting. Far more frequently, a company's core values make the headlines after something has gone very wrong (as we looked at early on). In so many cases, the folks with responsibility for leading their organizations and exemplifying the values that should serve as a strong foundation don't take the time to build them into their daily routines—talking about them or modeling them—and task the HR or marketing departments with creating some flashy slogan with hopes that this will be all it takes for the values to cascade down through the ranks.

> **I can only list a handful of companies that I've seen do more than list their values in a handbook or briefly mention those values in an occasional staff meeting.**

If we take shortcuts or get too fancy in the most challenging parts of building a home, we can expect significant issues at some point down the road. The same holds true for establishing the foundation for our organization around our core values; as difficult as it can be to avoid, taking shortcuts or getting fancy *will* lead to trouble. Sticking with the basics of establishing a foundation based on our core values won't likely be all that exciting, but we'll need to keep this very simple as we build those values into our routines.

Starting Off Simple Isn't Very Exciting

In the fifth lesson of our *Emerging Leader Development* course, I share a story about how a friend once introduced Cindy and me to some of his business partners. After a few seconds of puzzling out a reasonable description, he said, "They're *consistent*."

Since we still work very closely with that friend today, he's heard me use that example many times. Each time, he shakes his head and attempts to apologize for such a basic introduction. I always respond by telling him that it was one of the most heartwarming things we could have heard anyone say about us. While many people possess more talent and advanced formal education than either of us, I haven't met many who have been as consistent as Cindy and I have been since starting our business in 2015—or, honestly, in any of our previous roles.

When we're working, as leaders, to lay the initial foundation of values that we want our entire organization to be built on moving forward, we'll have no choice but to be highly consistent. I'll be very candid with you here: building that consistency is incredibly hard. But consistency is important enough that I created a lesson in our *Leading At The Next Level* program that outlined steps for developing a system for doing exactly that, based on our individual behavioral style. I assure you that the systems I use to help me remain consistent would offer little support for Cindy to do the same. And that's OK, because the systems that help her stay consistent in everything she does would likely cause me to have a seizure. It's not the individual steps that matter; it's the consistency we develop through those steps!

In detailing the process involved in laying the foundation for any kind of building, I mentioned being assigned to the crew doing that work, because I lacked the fine-tuned skills to be proficient in the plumbing, electrical, or trim work. In addition to my rough carpentry skills, the other skill I developed at just fifteen years old was my work ethic. As I mentioned earlier, laying the foundation and installing the roof system are the most physically demanding stages I've experienced in building a home. Without a strong work ethic, I can't picture many teenagers sticking it out for the entire summer, especially if they're riding a bicycle to and from work while trying to keep up with men who have worked in that trade for most of their lives. Although there's little excitement involved with digging or pouring footers, mixing mud and laying cinder blocks, setting trusses, or nailing down asphalt shingles (all by hand in those days), the simple steps involved with each are hard, and each must be completed effectively and consistently. Even the slightest shortcut to streamline the work could have a tremendous negative impact years down the road.

As leaders, modeling the values that will serve as our organization's foundation requires the same hard, consistent effort. Developing a system to incorporate each behavior that exemplifies one of our values into our everyday routine—especially if we can design that system around our individual behavioral style—can be the difference between getting a strong start and sustaining it over the long haul. I heard the phrase "Work smarter, not harder" repeatedly while learning to pour concrete. I was trying to muscle my way through the process, and at 130 pounds, there wasn't much muscle to use! The guys I worked with made it seem almost effortless, because they had developed systems for doing that backbreaking work. Teaching me their systems may have been nearly as difficult as working with the concrete. Getting our team members to follow suit in modeling our values can seem challenging early on, which makes it even more important to keep things as simple as possible.

Flashy May Get Attention, but Simple Sticks

For the first several years Cindy and I provided our *Emerging Leader Development* course for individuals and organizations, I was adamant that I DID NOT want to market any type of "coaching" tied to that course or anything else we offered. I had seen so many charlatans embed themselves into different organizations' cost structures by whispering some sweet nothings in a decision maker's ear (and the occasional smooch on that same decision maker's backside) without delivering any measurable return on investment that I wanted as much distance as we could get between that and the value I knew we were providing.

We've always been intentional about challenging each participant to identify the specific action steps they would apply from each lesson in the *Emerging Leader Development* course, as well as any other lesson we shared, and to provide those action steps to their immediate manager so they could work together on implementing and sustaining them to capture increased profitability.

The problem we soon encountered was that some of those managers never acknowledged the action steps that were sent to them. For time's sake, I'll stay off that soapbox, but you can imagine the message this sent those participants who had just detailed how they planned to lead their teams more effectively, yet received no response.

It's no secret that Cindy is much smarter than I am. Through all my pontification about why I didn't want to connect the term *coaching* to our business model, she politely listened. After seeing several outstanding folks work through courses with us yet struggle to stick with the subsequent action steps they hoped to put in place, she gently suggested we begin including one-on-one packages to work directly with these participants after they completed a course. We would help them implement, tweak, and sustain what they had learned—and do it in a way we could help them measure improvements in productivity and profitability—in cases where their managers or owners didn't have the time to do that themselves. We weren't coming up with the action steps; we were supporting them as they built these new behaviors into their daily routines. As much as I didn't want to admit it, we were indeed *coaching*, but in a way that made a positive impact on each organization's bottom line.

Here's the reality: adopting any new process or system, whether it's EOS, Lean Manufacturing, or another proven methodology, requires effort and commitment. Sustaining that change over time, while managing the demands of leading a team, can be a significant challenge. Systems like EOS, as outlined in Gino Wickman's *Traction*, or Lean Manufacturing, which built on principles championed by W. Edward Deming decades ago, are powerful tools that can drive remarkable results. These approaches have helped countless organizations streamline operations, align teams, and achieve their goals. However, their success hinges on one critical factor: the discipline to consistently apply them in alignment with the organization's core values.

The allure of a new system can generate excitement, but without a strong foundation, even the best methodologies can falter. It's not about the system itself being groundbreaking; it's about how leaders integrate it into their daily routines. Cindy and I often ask those we coach, "What would I see you doing differently if I worked for you?" This question helps leaders clarify the specific, practical behaviors needed to bring a system to life. More importantly, we encourage them to keep it simple. A simple approach, rooted in core values, is easier to sustain and delivers long-term impact.

Focusing on simple, value-driven routines may not grab headlines or feel flashy, but it's what creates resilience. When challenges arise—and they always do—those core values and disciplined habits provide the bandwidth to stay the course. Rather than chasing the latest trend or adding unnecessary complexity, leaders who model their organization's values consistently build a foundation that supports sustainable success, no matter the methodology they choose. With that in mind, let's explore how straightforward routines, grounded in your core values, can empower you and your team to thrive, even in the toughest moments.

Strong Habits Create Capacity for Adjustments

I was able to observe most of the practices while our son wrestled. It was interesting to watch how the best coaches had those kids go through new techniques repeatedly, slowly, until each movement became almost natural. During the few times I've dropped by my friend's mixed martial arts gym, I've noticed him applying the same approach in how he teaches Brazilian Jiu-Jitsu and Muay Thai. The way Cindy and I prepare for delivering a keynote presentation isn't wildly different, aside from the fact that our preparation isn't full-contact. We do, however, work through the material we'll be presenting over and over and over again!

In each of these examples, developing "muscle memory" plays a significant role in game-time performance. The more we practice something we've learned, the better our chances are of sustaining it over time. Keeping things simple definitely helps it stick. Make no mistake, though, I'm not suggesting that practice alone will lead to perfect execution; that's nonsense! Therein lies the importance of getting a second set of eyes on how we're taking action and continuously improving our technique—be that in sports, in making a presentation, or in basically any role. Whether it's from our manager or a trusted coach, refining how we practice a new behavior has an ongoing impact on the results we achieve. And when our manager or coach is focused on helping us achieve the best results we're capable of, they'll also emphasize the value of simplicity over flashiness.

All this ties directly to something I learned through my time in behavior-based safety: the majority of what we do each day is based on our habits. Those habits, the routine things we do throughout our day with little or no thought, account for a significant amount of the total results we achieve—good or bad. The longer we've performed each task a certain way, the more difficult it can be to make a change initially. Sustaining that change requires creating a new habit. Statistically, this involves maintaining a new behavioral pattern for 21 to 30 days without reverting to our previous behavior.

Practicing a new technique slowly in any combat sport is significantly different from executing it effectively in a match. The work Cindy and I do in our respective offices to prepare for a keynote presentation is a world apart from delivering that message once we're mic'd up in front of hundreds of people.

A friend serving in the United States Army once told me that "even the best battle plan goes to hell with the first shot fired down range." In battle, in combat sports, when delivering a presentation, AND even when we're working to lay a foundation on our company's core values, developing habits for how we perform each behavior involved provides us with additional bandwidth to make any necessary adjustments when that first shot goes down range. When we know precisely what exemplifying that behavior looks like and we've practiced enough to execute it without thinking about it, we have the capacity to make slight adjustments based on the situation we're in at the time.

> **Developing habits for how we perform each behavior involved provides us with additional bandwidth to make any necessary adjustments.**

I watched Matt develop the ability to perform moves (and countermoves) intuitively while wrestling once he had built that muscle memory. The more fluid Cindy and I can be in the material we're sharing with a group, the more we're able to tailor every word to the people in each audience—even when we've just met them moments before we begin the presentation. Becoming crystal-clear about the behaviors we need to practice while modeling our core values then repeating those behaviors consistently, is exactly how we create the habits that ensure those values are a visible part of our daily routine.

Creating these habits will not be flashy; we've got to keep things simple. However, that will most certainly not be *easy*, and it will likely be tedious.

Keeping Things Simple Isn't Easy

Just as laying a foundation for a building to stand the test of time requires work, establishing routines that model the core values that will ultimately serve as the foundation of our organization can be incredibly difficult. Before moving on, I've got to ask: is it just me, or does it always seem to be way harder to develop good habits than it is to slip into bad ones? I suppose we could take a lesson from what Robert Frost shared more than 100 years ago in "The Road Not Taken[28]." Slipping into habits that don't exemplify our values is far easier than doing what it takes to be the example we want our teams to follow.

While it's been a long time since I've dug or poured footers or mixed mud for block layers, I still have a vivid memory of exactly what's required in each step of a residential foundation, none of which is particularly exciting. Establishing the habits needed to effectively live out our organizational values, especially when starting from scratch and being the only one working to do so, is a heavy load for even the strongest leader. But practicing the behavior to develop the habit isn't the most challenging part; the step before and the step after both require even more determination.

Early in this process, we examined the importance of removing any possible ambiguity and defining exactly what the words we list as our core values truly mean. As you can imagine, Cindy and I work closely with many of our clients to help ensure they've done both. Developing a clear and concise definition for how each value is understood organizationally is a critical starting point, but it's only a starting point! As leaders, we need to identify exactly how each of those definitions apply to our daily responsibilities; we need to translate them to the behaviors our teams see us performing. Developing that level of clarity for how we model each value may sound *simple*, but I assure you it's not *easy*.

> **As leaders, we need to identify exactly how each of those definitions apply to our daily responsibilities; we need to translate them to the behaviors our teams see us performing.**

With that firm mental picture for acting out each value, we can get to work on establishing our routine; our habits. Systems for sticking with each behavior until we've created the muscle memory I referenced before are huge, especially when we build those systems to support our individual behavioral style. Even then, there will be times when it feels like we're not gaining any ground, when doing the same old simple things isn't making a difference. We'll constantly hear about this new fad or that new approach, each being touted as the best thing since sliced bread. The urge to chase new rabbits will often be high, but do you know what happens when you chase multiple rabbits? You don't catch any.

Consistency, of course, is rarely exciting. Even more so when we're working to keep our routines as simple as possible so each team member looking to us for leadership can understand precisely why we're doing what we're doing and how they can follow suit. I'll repeat it: keeping things simple isn't easy. And many times, it's just plain boring. Eventually, though, our teams will catch on. For that to happen, we'll need to be very clear in detailing why we've chosen our simple approach and how each of them can achieve the same results.

Detailing Why, Over and Over...

As we wrapped up our look at who ultimately cares about our values and how much our organization's entire reputation rests on them, I emphasized the importance of modeling our values and explaining why—because we can't just assume the general public will piece it all together on their own; they're busy chasing their own rabbits. Truth be told, we need to be just as intentional about providing that same kind of detail for everyone inside our organizations, too.

Over the last few years, Cindy and I have shared a lesson called "Building Buy-In Around a Clear Mission & Vision" with over a thousand leaders from several hundred companies across the United States. In that message, we emphasize that each team member be not only familiar with the company's mission and vision statements (which are often displayed prominently in the lobby for the world to see) but also has clarity on how their individual responsibilities contribute to achieving the mission and vision. We hit on values during that session as well, but the reality is that values have to be firmly in place at every level of our organization to have any chance of sustaining the behaviors necessary for achieving the mission and vision.

> **Values have to be firmly in place at every level of our organization to have any chance of sustaining the behaviors necessary for achieving the mission and vision.**

The challenge I often see leaders struggle with is feeling like they're beating a dead horse as they repeatedly include specifics about their values, whether in routine one-on-one conversations or larger settings with their entire teams. When it comes to our values, though, there's no such thing as talking about them too much!

Twice to this point, as we looked at ways we can rally our team around our values and again when working through how we model our values for everyone to see, I mentioned something in passing that many of us likely take for granted today, at least those of us who have come to love God's chicken sandwich. In yet another conversation with Jeff Henderson, who worked directly for Truett Cathy earlier in his career, he shared the story behind the "My Pleasure" that you and I have become so dependent on as we wrap up our short stint in line at Chick-fil-A. Before I move on, though, do you know what happens when a Chick-fil-A employee forgets to say that today? Do yourself a favor and check that out on YouTube.

Jeff shared that Mr. Cathy had his own initial "My Pleasure" experience while staying at a Ritz Carlton. Truett said it just felt better than hearing the traditional "You're welcome" or, even worse, "No problem," after thanking someone for their service. That was one of many things that set his experience apart from stays at other hotels, prompting him to begin working on implementing the phrase within the Chick-fil-A culture. Let's be honest: receiving that "My Pleasure" response feels a lot better than having someone grunt "No problem" when we get the wrong food, without a milkshake, after being held hostage for a week and a half in the McDonald's drive-through.

As he is the founder of the company that brought us God's chicken sandwich, and the builder of a culture that provides an experience previously unheard of in the fast food sector, one could easily assume that, when he so much as suggested the idea of replacing "You're welcome" with "My Pleasure," the heavens opened and every single person even remotely affiliated with the organization fell right in line. But one would be wrong!

From the time he first shared the idea internally, it took Truett Cathy ten full years of explaining exactly why he wanted the Chick-fil-A organization to be known that way. Not only did he have to model a seemingly simple request routinely himself, but he also had to provide explicit details on how, when, and why each team member should use that response themselves. But ten years? Holy cow! (get it, the Chick-fil-A cow!)

Galatians 6:9[29] says, "Let us not be weary in well doing: for in due season we shall reap *IF* we faint not." Drive past any Chick-fil-A around lunchtime, and it's easy to see that the Cathy family, as well as the owner of each store, has made it to that "due season" part. Had Truett let up on his expectation for "My Pleasure" to be the automatic response to any version of "Thank you" after even nine years, it may not be what we're accustomed to today.

If it took him that long for this to permeate his company, isn't it fair to expect we'll need to be willing to pound the drum over and over, detailing why we've chosen the behaviors we use to model our values, and exactly how each team member can do the same while fulfilling their responsibilities? Keeping it simple helps us get the ball rolling. Explaining it clearly will be a difference-maker in whether our teams internalize our message.

Specific Detail, Shared Simply and Clearly

While the foundation for the residential construction projects from my teens was on a much smaller scale than the aforementioned skyscrapers, they were no less critical to the long-term stability of the home. The same holds true for the core values of any business, regardless of its size. Although rarely exciting to start simple and detail exactly why we've chosen those values, especially when we're the only ones engaged in that process early on (or for years in some cases), it's just as essential as the strong foundation in the construction world.

In *Everyone Communicates, Few Connect*[30], while emphasizing the importance of keeping things simple as one of the core practices for leaders to connect with their teams, John Maxwell quotes Albert Einstein, "If you can't explain it simply, you don't understand it enough." During a recent session that Cindy and I hosted for owners and executives from approximately twenty organizations with which we work closely, a significant portion of the conversation centered on how many organizations list the same words as their core values without clearly differentiating what is expected in practice at any level. Reflecting on the eloquent definitions of Enron that we examined early on, the general ideas were clear, but there was minimal specificity regarding how those values would be displayed in any particular role.

One key lesson I've learned from leading through difficult situations is that, when we don't provide clarity as quickly as possible, our teams are left to form their own conclusions. And, like it or not, those conclusions are often based on assumptions derived from limited information, viewed through a lens focused solely on their individual scope of work. This is the epitome of the phrase, "You can't see the picture when you're in the frame."

> **When we don't provide clarity as quickly as possible, our teams are left to form their own conclusions.**

Without providing explicit clarity on how they apply to any given team member's role, even the most brilliantly crafted definition will be insufficient to guide those team members in adapting our values to their behaviors on their own. Whether it's because we don't feel like we have the time to provide that level of detail, or we think we've already explained it well enough, or we don't have enough familiarity with what's involved in their daily tasks to do it, failing to share this kind of clarity leaves the door wide open to them coming up with a mismatched definition— if they're still thinking about those values at all.

Defining our values simply, and detailing the behaviors involved in displaying them in each team member's role, will never be easy. It is, however, our responsibility—if we hope ever to have our core values embedded as deeply within our company as "My Pleasure" is with Chick-fil-A. Even then, we'll need to become an individual case study of displaying something I've suggested a few times to this point: *consistency*.

CHAPTER EIGHT

BUILDING A CULTURE AROUND VALUES: A CONSISTENT EXAMPLE

Think back to what I referenced before about companies having wonderfully crafted mission and vision statements framed majestically in their lobbies. Here's the AI overview I got from typing "mission, vision, culture, values" in the Google[31] search bar:

> A "mission" defines an organization's core purpose and reason for existence, a "vision" outlines the desired future state of the company, "culture" represents the shared behaviors and beliefs within an organization, and "values" are the guiding principles that shape the company's decision-making and actions, all working together to create a unified identity and direction.

Having recently published *Leading With A Clear Purpose*, I'm over the moon with that connection between a mission statement and an organization's core (or even *clear*) purpose. And who doesn't appreciate a well-defined vision for where their organization is headed? Our culture, though, is most definitely a representation of what's going on day-to-day, the behaviors used by the team as a whole, rather than something referenced on a website or TV ad. However, the foundation for all of these things is truly built on the core values we, as leaders, have modeled and explained long enough for each team member to understand exactly how they can apply them in their own role—and then do so regularly.

To have a realistic chance of our mission or vision resonating externally, or for the internal culture of our team to be the driving force behind that mission and vision, it is essential to detail and exemplify our core values. We'll need to keep it simple for any hope of being applied, but it's nothing short of imperative that the example we provide is one of the most consistent things in our team members' lives. We will indeed be responsible for discussing our organization's core values every chance we get, and that will be a good start.

If you have kids, or you've ever been around a kid at any point in your life, you know they pay far more attention to what we do than what we say. Not sure? Let a swear word slip in front of them, then tell them not to repeat it. Do they follow your instructions, or do they follow your example? In studying human behavior for more than two decades, whether it relates to workplace safety or how we communicate with one another, I've come to realize that age has little to do with the behaviors we choose. As much as I'd love to suggest that maturity plays a key role, I think about all the times I've heard John Maxwell say, "Maturity comes with age, but sometimes age comes alone."

The most significant driver behind how we choose our behaviors, which form our habits as we repeat them over time, is the consequence we anticipate achieving (or receiving) from that behavior. We'll delve into how to manage those consequences from a leadership perspective soon effectively. For now, let's stick with something we have far more direct control over, which plays a close second when working to guide behavior throughout our teams (or even with our kids): the *consistent* example they see from us.

As important as it is for us to provide a simple explanation of how our values can be applied in each role, it won't be enough for our team members to see us model them occasionally. They need to be able to see that example every single time they look to us.

Your Culture is Counting On You!

Before a potential wound festers, let's ensure we clean it properly. I occasionally ruffle feathers when I compare the actions our team members take to those of our children. I don't mean that to be in the least belittling. I'm at least as capable of doing something immature (and sometimes just plain stupid) as anyone you'll ever meet. And as I've grown into a bit of a grumpy old man (on occasion), I've noticed the limited filter I had developed over the years doesn't always work quite like it used to.

Please understand, though, that I'm not alone in suggesting that adults are often motivated like kids. Still, I do always attempt to tie it back to behavioral science rather than just being mean. Here's a statement I found from a Forbes.com article called "Leadership Tips: Setting the Example[32]," making a similar comparison while emphasizing just how important it is for every leader to exemplify what they need from their teams:

> "As a leader, you find yourself in a position previously held by kindergarten teachers and the cool kids of our high schools: the example-setter, the person that others look to for acceptable behavior. Rather than clothes or music, you're demonstrating to those who follow how the attitude with which to approach their jobs and each other. It might be a responsibility that you feel is unwanted, or unnecessary; again, everyone working for you is an adult, and should be able to make their own determinations as to how they need to work to be successful. But, we all gather cues from those in our proximity that can affect our thoughts and behavior, and it's the job of a leader to try and sway them in a positive direction."

> **As a leader, you find yourself in a position previously held by kindergarten teachers and the cool kids of our high schools: the example-setter, the person that others look to for acceptable behavior.**

As leaders, it's nothing short of mandatory that we consistently demonstrate the core values of our organization. We'd do well to follow what John Maxwell defines in chapter nine of *The 17 Indisputable Laws of Teamwork*[33] as "The Law of Countability." John explains that "teammates must be able to count on each other when it counts" and provides further detail by sharing, "If there is a breakdown in countability, then the account is lost, the customer goes away unhappy, and the job goes to some other candidate."

To build a culture around our values, we have no choice but to be countable if we're leading anyone at all. Our team members must be able to count on *us* when it comes to the values we want to count! John also tied *countability* to character, quoting Barry Gibbons, from his book *This Indecision Is Final*[34], as saying, "Write and publish what you want, but the only mission, values, and ethics that count in your company are those that manifest themselves in the behavior of all the people, all the time."

That, my friend, is our culture. And our culture will be built on the consistent example we provide, showing how our core business values can be modeled in each role; our culture will be built on the example our teams *count* on us to deliver. I'll say it once more: Keeping things simple isn't easy. Throughout *What's KILLING Your Profitability?* and *Leading With A Clear Purpose*, I was intentional in emphasizing that leadership at any level is challenging. In fact, the author of that Forbes article closed with this:

> "Setting the example isn't easy; it requires you to be always on, always living up to the standard you want for others. And even then we can fall short with a bad day, an off day. But the key is getting your team to understand the ideal that you strive for, and the values and culture that you're looking to instill, while accepting that everyone, even you, will fall short from time to time. What matters is that they keep striving towards that ideal."

Even through some bumps in the road, our consistent, *countable* example is a key part of building our values into the organizational culture. However, we'll still need to discuss them just as consistently, and we'll need to connect all of this to what each team member does in their own role.

Have You Gotten Through (Yet)?

In the fourth lesson of our *Emerging Leader Development* course, Cindy and I detail five critical practices for effective communication. In that process, we emphasize just how important it is that we keep our message simple and share it over and over and over again with absolute consistency. Cindy often relates this need for consistency to the marketing adage that we need to see or hear a message at least seven times before it sticks.

While covering that lesson with an organization several years ago, I asked everyone in the group who had kids to raise their hands. I challenged those with their hands raised to equate that to how often they had to say something to their kids before it sunk in. The CEO immediately responded by saying, "I'll let you know as soon as it happens." After we all had a good laugh, I asked how old his children were. He shared that they were all grown and had kids of their own, but still didn't seem to pay much attention to what he told them. I'll say it once more: our behavior as adults isn't all that different from our behavior as children.

In many cases, I'll apologize when I pound the same drum repeatedly while making a point. This IS NOT one of those cases! The people we lead are counting on us to model our core company values consistently. They're counting on us to provide explicit details about how our behavior exemplifies those values. And, whether or not we ever realize it, they're counting on us to connect all of that directly to the tasks they're responsible for daily.

> **The people we lead are counting on us to model our core company values consistently.**

Through the second part of *Leading With A Clear Purpose*, I challenge readers with responsibility for leading teams to not only help each of their team members identify a clear purpose that inspires them to charge hell with a water pistol every day but to provide those team members with everything they need to connect their individual purpose to the clear purpose they're working to achieve as an organization.

I'm not suggesting that's an easy task. It's not! And that's why I dedicated several chapters to detailing specific steps a leader can take to fulfill that need for their team members.

We must keep the behaviors that embody our values as simple as possible. We'd better be willing to detail why we're doing what we do for at least as long as Truett Cathy was for "My Pleasure." However, as leaders it still rests on us to consistently connect those values to what each of our team members can and should be doing daily. So let's work through the specifics of how we can do exactly that.

Do We Walk the Talk, Every Day?

Building a culture around values requires the leader to provide a daily example of exactly how each definition outlined in the handbook and on the wall directly applies to what's required of them. Providing a detailed explanation, connecting those definitions to their behaviors so nothing is left to assumption, is just as important. Based on the MIT Sloan Management Review article I've cited a few times previously, stating that "more than three-quarters of CEOs interviewed in a major business magazine discussed their company's culture or core values — even when not specifically asked about it," the talking piece usually happens (even if it's only to the reporters or investors). Even when we're intentional about having those conversations with the team members counting on us for that clarity, and even when we're able to articulate clear ties between our own behaviors and how we've defined our core company values, that doesn't automatically mean any of it will translate to what each of them does in their own daily routine.

Through the *Strategic Leadership Coaching* that Cindy and I provide for dozens of business owners and executives today, we frequently challenge them to identify tasks that they're doing. Still, we may not need to—the tasks that someone on their team could take over, allowing them to have more time for things that only they can do. During these conversations, we always stress that it's not about *dumping* something we don't like onto someone as a form of punishment; this should be carefully thought out so that any responsibility *delegated* helps the team member develop their own skills in the process.

We frequently hear leaders say, "I won't ask someone to do something that I'm not willing to do myself." While we admire the spirit behind that, the stark reality of leadership is that we simply don't have enough hours in the day to do everything we are physically capable of doing or everything we want to do. All that said, ensuring everyone on our teams has a crystal-clear understanding of our core values IS NOT one of the things we can ever delegate (or *dump*).

In a recent interview about the release of *Leading With A Clear Purpose*, I was asked why I thought there were so many varying descriptions of "leadership" and to describe what it meant to me. I stated that I viewed "leadership" as a verb, the act of providing a service to others that they're not capable of themselves. I explained that authority had nothing to do with this kind of leadership. I went on to reference what I once heard Dave Ramsey share in detailing the difference between "servant leadership" and "subservient leadership." Dave said, "Subservient leadership is doing something for someone that they can and should be doing for themselves, whereas true servant leadership is doing what they cannot do to help them be even more effective in what they can do."

As we work to help our team members understand exactly how our core values can be modeled in their roles, there will be times when we should absolutely perform tasks that typically fall within their scope of work. And when we do, we must explain the connection between the word we hold us as a value and the behavior we've used to put it into practice—just like when we exemplify that value while doing our own work. Do we walk the talk in every way possible, and do we do it every day?

With that question in mind, here's one of the best examples of this that I've ever seen personally.

Nothing Left to Chance...

As we started down this path detailing how strong businesses are built on a foundation of values, I shared something I personally experienced while creating a policy manual for the new owners of the company—a textbook example of not just designing that handbook around their core values, but building those values into every decision they made while leading the organization.

Through the time I spent with Craig as we crafted the manual for his new team, I saw him exemplify the five values around which he and

Kim decided to build their company. Not only did I see him exhibit *compassion, integrity, humility, family,* and *dependability* while performing each of his own responsibilities, but I can't think of a time when I was at their place of business and didn't see Craig take advantage of opportunities to model how those values could be applied in other roles. Whether it was being compassionate in a situation with a teammate (where his predecessors would have been less understanding), showing genuine humility by carrying a purchase to a customer's car (rather than directing someone else to do it) or treating everyone he interacted with—included Cindy and me—like they were part of his family, everyone working there saw and felt those values for months before we detailed them in his new handbook. Each team member had ample opportunities to see how Craig expected the values to be displayed in their own roles. And quite honestly, the longest-tenured ones respected and appreciated his example even more than those who were newer on the team.

> **Each team member had ample opportunities to see how Craig expected the values to be displayed in their own roles.**

Just after their second anniversary of owning the business, Craig, Kim, and I had an initial conversation about adding a sixth value for at least one segment of their team: *visibility*. As we discussed it, Craig shared that he believed having each team member more intentional about their *visibility* with customers could yield as much as a five percent increase in that department's revenue. He went on to share something he experienced personally a few days prior. He saw an opportunity to be *visible* with a customer in their outdoor area, away from the more prevalent seasonal inventory where the rest of the team was focused. In less than fifteen minutes with that customer, he created a sale that represented *ten* percent of the entire day's business, a transaction that likely wouldn't have happened otherwise.

The three of us revisited the idea of adding *visibility* as their sixth core value a few weeks after that initial conversation. I asked if they had been discussing it regularly with their team. Craig shared that he had been emphasizing it so much that many of them were starting to joke about it; when calling for them on their walkie-talkies, they would respond by saying, "I'm out being *visible!*" As Truett Cathy had done in borrowing the "My Pleasure" idea from a high-end hotel, Craig and Kim related the concept of *visibility* to practices they had experienced in a Neiman Marcus store where associates took them directly to what they were looking for rather than telling them where to find it. They suggested that their team do the same *and*, at the same time, look for opportunities to answer other questions.

Craig shared with me that the company's overall revenue had grown by fifty percent—FIVE ZERO percent—in their first twenty-four months of ownership. More recently, the part of the business where *visibility* has been incorporated as its sixth value grew during a year with significant market challenges, while most of its direct competitors were down ten to fifteen percent from the previous year. The one clear difference I can point to has been how I've seen Craig, Kim, and now their entire leadership team living out their core values. They haven't left anything to chance; they're walking the talk every day! Even then, though, consistent reinforcement is crucial.

Consistent Examples Still Require Consistent Reinforcement

Even in cases where we leave absolutely nothing to chance, taking every single opportunity to provide examples showing how each of our core values can be acted upon in the roles our team members perform daily, we'll still need to provide consistent reinforcement backing our consistent example.

As I began this examination of the importance of our values, I mentioned the time involved in establishing or replacing a habit. Initially, that was specific to what we needed to do as leaders: to model our core values and keep them at the forefront of our team members' minds. Since then, I've mentioned how much more effort it takes to transform a one-time behavior into a habit that's part of our daily routine. Creating habits that align with our values in our own role is no small task, but helping our team members do the same, even after we've worked to show them exactly how, requires a very focused effort.

I alluded to our *Strategic Leadership Coaching* model when I shared how we challenge executives to delegate specific tasks to others within their organization. In transparency, I wanted absolutely nothing to do with "coaching," even though Cindy and I had both completed the certification process to offer that as a service. I had seen far too many clowns claiming to be coaches of this or that, but they had never accomplished anything themselves. Cindy, being so much more intelligent and much more intuitive than I, saw a tremendous need we could fill whereas I was stuck on the bullshit I had seen from other people.

Our goal in assigning "homework" after every lesson we deliver has always been to foster collaboration between the participant and their direct manager, enabling the manager to guide them in implementing their action steps and to help them sustain those steps long enough to form habits. When we realized that many of those managers weren't engaging their staff, even when they received extremely articulate lists of steps the participant hoped to implement after time with us, I finally conceded that Cindy had, once again, been right all along. We started providing "coaching" as a service—but with the specific goal of reinforcing the action steps they implemented, and capturing how those steps increased their productivity and profitability.

The important part isn't who's providing that reinforcement; it's that the behaviors modeling our core values are being recognized and routinely reinforced. As leaders, it's our responsibility to make sure that gets done. We are required to provide a clear understanding of what each value looks like in practice, as well as being an example every time we have the chance, but there's no way we can do it all on our own indefinitely—and we don't have to.

Moving forward, we'll work through specific steps to achieve this, whenever and however possible, and identify ways to engage the leaders around us in an active role in the process.

Building Consistent Team Behavior, Based on Our Values

Society has countless "influencers" with significant followings. Having a high number of people watch their foolishness online is vastly different from the responsibility leaders hold when they've earned genuine influence with the people on their teams, or for that matter, anyone whose behavior they impact. Whether we like it or not, walking the talk and providing a consistent example of what our core company values look like in application is imperative when we have this kind of influence on the people around us. Even when our behavior sets the proper tone for our teams, each team member will need routine reinforcement as they work to incorporate those values into their own tasks. And that will require feedback from us and everyone who's part of our leadership team. While this is anything but easy, it's far simpler than what we'll deal with indefinitely when those values aren't a consistent part of our entire team's behavior.

> **Walking the talk and providing a consistent example of what our core company values look like in application is imperative.**

My first direct reference to Chick-fil-A came from an article comparing their customer performance to McDonald's, with Chick-fil-A consistently ranking in the number one spot for ten consecutive years. With that ranking in mind, what do we all expect any time we visit one of their stores—anywhere? We expect to be waited on quickly and courteously. We expect to receive exactly what we ordered (which isn't likely to happen at any location with golden arches). We expect our food to be really good, and we can count on hearing "My Pleasure" several times. While I won't go so far as to suggest that any of these will be done perfectly every time, we can certainly bank on each of them being consistently executed well above average.

Before tying this to what you and I need to do to achieve this type of consistency with our team members modeling our core values, I'll remind you once more that it took Truett Cathy ten full years to thoroughly embed "My Pleasure" into the Chick-fil-A experience we count on today. We can learn from his success and build the behaviors that consistently model our company values into our team's routine in less time. To do that, we'll need to reference those values constantly and live the example we want our teams to follow.

We'll also need to set abundantly clear expectations for how their behavior should be based on our values.

Even when we've provided meticulous explanations, detailing exactly what we expect to see from that point forward and maintaining a high standard of accountability, we must continue to uphold this level of clarity.

The Non-Negotiables: We Can't Vary on Values

In chapter eight of *What's KILLING Your Profitability? (It ALL Boils Down to Leadership!)*, I detailed how much confusion costs an organization and emphasized the significant need for leaders to set crystal-clear expectations. Chapter nine fell right in line by outlining how much profitability is lost when teams aren't held accountable for at least meeting expectations. While both were geared towards overall performance, they're also crucial if we're to build consistent team behavior based on our core company values.

Setting abundantly clear expectations for modeling our values is a critical part of ensuring our organization's foundation leads to a lasting legacy, which we will explore in more detail soon. Before we get there, I'll challenge you to consider something that could be preventing your team from embracing your values as quickly, or in the way you had hoped.

In the nearly thirty years since Cindy and I started dating, we've come to realize that there are countless things we don't agree on. She thinks a ribeye needs to be all but burnt to be edible, and I prefer mine much like Sonny and Pepper ordered theirs in *A Cowboy Way*. Her approach to handling a problem is to think through several possible outcomes to identify the best way to achieve precision and accuracy on her first attempt, whereas I tend to go with the "hold my beer and watch this" approach (even though I don't drink), then make corrections as needed. I could go on like this for days, but hopefully, you're not the slow guy at the magic show, and you already get the point. While there are indeed many things we don't agree on, we realized early on that we didn't differ in our personal values. Loyalty to one another, our shared Faith, and an intense focus on character have been non-negotiables since the beginning of our relationship.

As leaders in our organizations, when we consistently talk about and model our core values, it's not about coercing our team members into being mindless clones who do exactly what we say because they have no other choice. The concept of diversity, equity, and inclusion has been in the headlines continuously for several years—and rarely for the right reasons. Since I toe the line by challenging the societal norm in the third lesson of our *Recruitment, Retention, & Culture* course, I'll only touch on it briefly here: the most powerful thing I've seen true diversity provide any organization is varying thought processes that drive genuine, continuous improvement. Make no mistake, though, as great as diversity in experience, skill, and thought can be, I'm in no way suggesting there's room for diversity in values.

> ## As great as diversity in experience, skill, and thought can be, I'm in no way suggesting there's room for diversity in values.

The reason I continue emphasizing the need for every leader to discuss their company's core values in explicit detail, and model those values daily, is that the only way we can hope to see our teams consistently display them is to demonstrate such values are non-negotiable. In *Traction*[35], Gino Wickman shares this in detailing how important organizational values are, "Once they're defined, you must hire, fire, review, and recognize people based on these core values. This is how to build a thriving culture around them."

> ## Once they're defined, you must hire, fire, review, and recognize people based on these core values. This is how to build a thriving culture around them.

When we consistently model our values in our own role, routinely discuss those values with our teams, and seize every opportunity to demonstrate how each value can be applied in our team members' actions, we should eventually see our teams following suit. We also need to recognize them for doing it.

Recognized Behavior Gets Repeated

Building consistent team behavior based on our core company values will require removing any possible variance in how each value is applied across each role. But having a clear understanding of the necessary behaviors is just part of the process. It will take at least as much effort for our team members to build those (likely) different behaviors into their routines as it did for us, maybe even more. As leaders, we will need to be very intentional about recognizing even the slightest changes we see them making.

> **It will take at least as much effort for our team members to build those (likely) different behaviors into their routines as it did for us, maybe even more.**

I reference the lessons I learned through my experience in behavior-based safety for multiple reasons. Of course, it's rewarding to help reduce workplace injuries, as well as the associated costs. That for fifteen years it was my primary responsibility for close resulted in that methodology being a part of who I am today. But maybe more important than either of those is how much it taught me about why we all do what we do, even though it was through a lens explicitly focused on safety. One core tenant I probably don't allude to enough: **recognized behavior gets repeated!**

I learned this in theory early on in my exposure to the world of behavior-based safety, but I discovered it in practice while tossing a baseball back and forth with our son when he was seven or eight years old. It was his first time wearing a glove, so that alone took some getting used to. Since I had always been extremely good at baseball (everything except the parts that required running, hitting, and catching), I was uniquely qualified to bark commands at a kid with zero perspective for what he should be doing. Each time he attempted to catch the ball, he held the glove like a basket. If the ball was coming from high above his head, that was fine. If it was coming straight at him, it was going to glance off his hand just prior to removing any remaining baby teeth.

As parents, what are we naturally inclined to do? For me, it was to address what he was doing wrong—over and over and over. And that recognized behavior was definitely getting repeated. Too busy bitching about what he wasn't doing right, what *I* failed to do consistently was show him precisely what he should do instead. I do remember a few instances where he held the glove correctly and caught the ball, but I failed to comment on that since I was so engaged in addressing the more frequent undesired behavior.

After what seemed like an eternity—and probably even longer for him—it struck me that I should recognize and reinforce any attempt he made to change how he held the glove, instead of only chastising him. Making that simple change didn't resolve the issue immediately, but it sure helped, and it made the entire experience something we both (eventually) enjoyed.

To build a culture around values, even after we've laid a simple foundation and walked the talk every day, we must ensure that we celebrate even the smallest victories with our team members as they work to model our company values in their daily routines. Those small victories, especially when recognized appropriately and consistently, will build to bigger victories.

All that said, we will still need to address instances where they fall short, but doing so requires the clear expectations I mentioned earlier. Having clear, sustainable expectations, and maintaining accountability for how we expect our core values to be exemplified, can build the legacy we want to achieve as an organization. That's what we'll work through next.

CHAPTER NINE

CREATING A LEGACY THROUGH VALUES: SUSTAINABLE EXPECTATIONS

Once we've laid a foundation around the simple practices involved in modeling our core company values, and we've provided our teams with a consistent example of what living out each value looks like, we should be well on our way to building the culture we're after within our organization. However, creating a legacy that leaves a positive impression on anyone who ever hears about us—the reputation we're known for, far and wide, and long after we're gone—will require everyone on our team to exemplify those values. To achieve this, we must establish clear expectations that can be sustained in the long term. This is how we can work toward our own version of Truett Cathy's "My pleasure!"

As I emphasized the importance of identifying the ways we can build our values into our daily routines, I also suggested we work to keep this as simple as possible, and tie any systems we create back to how we're wired individually—our own behavioral style. To ensure it sinks in, I'll stress this again: flashy ideas and fancy new approaches may draw attention initially, but simplicity drives results. We'll never get lasting value from something we can't stick with!

To build our business on a foundation of values that truly have a lasting impact on the people we're called to serve, sustainable expectations are essential. While this certainly isn't complicated, we'll need to be incredibly intentional in how we go about it. As with modeling our core values through our own behavior, we'll set the standard for how every leader on our team defines what's expected and how they maintain accountability. If we can't sustain this, is it reasonable to think anyone on our team will?

With that in mind, let's take a detailed look at how we can establish high but sustainable expectations, communicate them clearly, and develop the kind of team accountability that everyone strives to live up to—rather than an atmosphere of threat-based compliance. In explaining "The Cost of Confusion" (chapter eight in *What's KILLING Your Profitability?*) I shared how I've frequently seen supervisors and managers shy away from setting high expectations for their teams, fearful this could push people away. The best leaders I've experienced not only set high expectations, but also hold their teams accountable for the behaviors required to achieve those expectations.

While complainers and mediocre performers were quick to distance themselves from this, it attracted some of the best team members in their organizations. And it all started with those leaders being crystal-clear about what was expected every single day.

Defining EXACTLY What's Expected

One of the most valuable lessons I've learned from John Maxwell over the last decade or so was from a short session I had access to just before the larger event where I completed certification to teach and train on his material. John shared a brief lesson before fielding questions for the small group. But before taking those questions, since we would all soon be newly licensed to represent the content he had poured his life into, John told us that he needed us to be very intentional about consistently exceeding our client's expectations any time we were using his name. He went on to explain that the only way we could ever have the slightest chance of doing this was by making sure we understood exactly what was expected. That requires clarity, clarity that we'll need to provide for each of our team members if we hope they'll work alongside us in creating a legacy through our organization's core values.

I can't speak for the rest of the folks in that room, but hearing John Maxwell place that expectation on us added a tremendous amount of pressure on me. Having studied his work for close to fifteen years at that point, I'd learned as much from him as I had from any other source, and I had a high level of respect for his resources. Before delving into further detail on how we explain the behaviors we expect to see in modeling our values, I'll share what John said as he wrapped up, which immediately removed a load of stress.

As vital as it was for us to work to exceed expectations, he noted, doing so would immediately separate us from even the closest competition. He went on to share that, in his experience, 80% of people routinely fall short of what is expected. Around 15% of the population will typically do just what they're expected to, then stop. And only 5% will ever work to go beyond what's expected. John concluded by detailing how simply taking the time to understand what a client is looking for gives us the opportunity to exceed their expectations.

Unfortunately, I'm convinced that his percentages are no longer accurate; it seems like far more than 80% fall short of what's expected, and finding those who exceed expectations has become increasingly rare. Most of us in the room with John back then were already in leadership roles or running our own businesses. As leaders, it truly falls on our shoulders to ensure we understand exactly what is expected of us from anyone we provide with any service, however slight. When we have a team counting on us for leadership, we're also responsible for providing them with explicit details of what they're expected to do—including how we expect them to model our core values. As I mentioned earlier, I often see people shy away from setting (or maintaining) high expectations for their teams, concerned about pushing away those with critical skills. Generally, the opposite is the case. Failing to set clear—and high—expectations allows room for mediocre performance and frustrates our best team members. While high expectations may weed out underperformers, they tend to bring out the best in others. Great team members are consistently ready and willing to exceed expectations, and that sets the tone for outstanding team performance, sustainably aligned with our values.

> **Failing to set clear—and high—expectations allows room for mediocre performance and frustrates our best team members.**

Great Teams Are Built Around High Expectations

I remember a time very early in my behavior-based safety career when Terry Ward (who I've mentioned several times in this look at values and throughout my first two books) stopped by my office to chat about something. When he stepped in, I had an email pulled up from Cindy. I don't recall what the exchange was about, but it was likely something related to our son and one of his teachers. Regardless, it wasn't work-related.

Terry called me out on it. He wasn't rude; he was just direct. He was also very intentional in explaining the perception that could give anyone else coming into my office. Our behavior-based safety initiative was still relatively new, and lacked support from many of his peers on the management team. To take it a step further, he shared some examples of others in the facility who had developed habits of addressing that sort of business on company time, who had earned reputations for being less than stellar performers.

He closed by saying that while he understood the reason, he still expected me to take the high road and set a great example. Remember the lesson about choosing the harder right over the easier wrong that I learned from him and his time at West Point?

Here's the kicker: Terry wasn't my boss. On paper, he had no positional authority to give me direction. Quite honestly, my supervisor probably wouldn't have said a word about the email exchange with Cindy. I was effective in my role and hadn't dropped the ball on any of the tasks I was required to complete. Terry, however, from the very first time I met him, has always had very high expectations of me. That was definitely the case the entire time we worked for the same company, but it hasn't changed in the nearly two decades since.

The most recent example was November of 2019, when Cindy and I visited him at his home in Richmond. He put his arm around me, told me how proud he was of several things we had accomplished, then proceeded to tell me I was fat—and he was 100% correct!

Since he was never my boss, why has his input carried so much weight in my life and career for more than 25 years? Very early on in our working relationship, he clearly and earnestly demonstrated his dedication to helping me grow. While he wasn't my supervisor or manager, I've always viewed him as an outstanding leader. Because he had earned that level of influence, I've always wanted to meet and exceed any expectations he has placed on me. Even when those expectations seemed out of reach, I pushed toward them, because I knew he wouldn't challenge me with something I wasn't capable of.

> **Because he had earned that level of influence, I've always wanted to meet and exceed any expectations he has placed on me.**

Now, let's tie all that to how we can work with our teams to create a legacy by living our company's core values. We've defined exactly what that looks like. The fact that you've stuck with me through this process assures me that you're likely going to do everything in your power to be in that 5% Maxwell said consistently exceeds expectations.

Think about the folks you've looked to for leadership throughout your career. Hold on, though: don't confuse that with any old clown who happened to have the word "manager" in his title; I'm talking about the ones who genuinely earned influence with you, as Terry did with me. If they set an expectation for you, one that you felt was even remotely possible, what were you willing to do to reach it? I'm betting anything you possibly could, and maybe a little more...

When a leader has earned our trust, we feel confident that any expectations they set are achievable; any expectations they place on us are ones we know can be sustained—even if they seem out of reach initially. And when those who have earned actual leadership influence consistently provide an example of how we can rise to their expectations, it brings out the best in us. Over time, setting high expectations for modeling our core values will bring together our best team players to form a great team.

Even then, though, accountability for sustaining those expectations is critical for creating a durable and honorable legacy.

Expectations Are Empty Talk without Accountability

To have a real shot at creating the legacy we hope for, based on our core company values, the expectations we set must be sustainable. Realistically, though, we wouldn't place unsustainable expectations on anyone we genuinely care about—and that should cover everyone we've earned influence with who's following us, regardless of our level of authority. That said, even the clearest of expectations are just talk if we're not willing to maintain a high level of accountability.

Think about it: how often have you seen a parent barking orders at their out-of-control child with no change in behavior whatsoever afterward—from the child or the parent? If you've ever spent more than ten minutes in a Walmart, I'm sure you've witnessed this plenty of times. (I haven't had to offer to spank someone's kid for them since we started using the grocery pickup option!) With that fresh in your mind, what do we naturally assume about that parent's relationship with their child? I realize there are exceptions, but it typically tells me that the child hasn't been held accountable for not following directions. Certainly I'm not suggesting that the parent has to jerk the kid out of the cart and beat them right there, but I've rarely seen a child who's held accountable running wild in Walmart.

So, how does that relate to setting sustainable expectations for how our team members embody our core values in their daily routines? Have you ever seen a coworker who is habitually late, even though the policy is very clear about when they're supposed to arrive? Have you ever been given a date for when something you've requested would be in your hands, only to have the individual who set the date repeatedly reset their own projection before coming through with what they committed to?

Just like any kid forced to endure the torture that is a trip through Walmart, all of us have bad days. However, when undesirable behavior from a team member or service provider is the norm, it's often because they haven't been held accountable for even meeting expectations, let alone exceeding them.

> **When undesirable behavior**
> **from a team member or service provider is the norm,**
> **it's often because they haven't been held accountable**
> **for even meeting expectations.**

As with the out-of-control kid in the store, the case I'm making here isn't for harsh and immediate discipline—although discipline certainly has its place in the equation, and we'll get to that soon. Accountability begins with calmly addressing behaviors that have fallen short of our expectations, detailing the necessary changes, and explaining what the future will hold if these changes are not made. In the example I shared before, Terry wasn't my manager, so he wasn't in a position to issue me a formal corrective action. But had I blown off the expectations he'd set for me, he could have easily stopped the investment he was making in my career development, and that would have been more detrimental than a write-up going in my file!

Whether we've truly earned the influence necessary to *lead* our teams authentically, or we're still working in that direction and have to *manage* performance actively, holding our team members accountable to live out our core values through what we expect from their daily behavior is an absolute necessity if we want to reach such a sustainable level. Accountability isn't something we can think about only when we've hit our boiling point because someone has missed the mark one too many times; it has to be in place every single day, and with every individual on our team.

Consistent Accountability - Across the Board

As I shared in the next-to-last chapter of *Leading With A Clear Purpose*, the compliance side of human resources drains the life out of me. Putting together employee handbooks, especially those where values are often listed in the first few pages but have little relevance to anything else afterward, drained me the fastest. Through the process, however, I was still able to learn some valuable lessons.

Early on, one of the managers I was working with to create a handbook commented on how detrimental it can be to include canned work rules we knew would never be administered. Having a policy that expressly prohibits profanity while supervisors use the most profane language imaginable to simply say 'good morning' not only removes any teeth from that policy, it also discredits every other work rule listed throughout the manual. The manager challenged me to consider that with any update we suggested. This wasn't just a question of whether it would be a viable change, but whether there was a realistic chance that the supervisors and managers throughout our facility would hold themselves or their teams accountable.

Soon after that conversation, I took over the majority of that facility's unemployment claim hearings. One of my responsibilities in disputing claims was to demonstrate that our management team had consistently followed the written policy, as evidenced by their actions with other team members before the situation in question. If I didn't have the documentation to prove our case, the company would be on the losing end of the claim even if the employee had genuinely violated policies repeatedly. Just as I shared earlier in my lesson from my time in behavior-based safety, any behavior that's recognized or rewarded is indeed repeated.

When it comes to those oh-so-important core company values, establishing and maintaining accountability is paramount. Not only do we need to exemplify those values in everything we do, but every manager and supervisor within our organization must do the same.

Yet that's not where it stops. The folks with those titles are not the only ones in our organization who have earned influence; our most senior and highly skilled team members have developed influence with the folks around them—positive or negative—and they're likely the ones who have the most interaction with those team members daily, too. If they step outside the lines on living out the company's values and we don't address it, we're endorsing, by default, that subpar behavior, not just with them but with everyone who's watching.

All too often, I've seen supervisors and managers turn a blind eye to a highly skilled team member who has fallen short. Sometimes, they justify this by saying that the behavior only occurs occasionally. Many times, though, they avoid the issue out of concern that addressing it will cause the team member to quit. Regardless of the reason, the message conveyed is that any expectation we've previously set for modeling our values is essentially empty talk. Although this won't likely result in our values being completely blown off immediately, each time we fail to maintain accountability perpetuates a downward spiral.

I've emphasized this with dozens, if not hundreds, of supervisors, managers, and executives over the last two decades: consistent accountability must be the norm for everyone in our organization. Unfortunately, many of them initially perceive my push for maintaining accountability as an insistence on proceeding directly to formal disciplinary action, and they do everything they can to avoid it. That's not the case I'm making, at least not at first.

Coaching, Not Condemnation

Creating a legacy through our core values requires us to set clear (and high) expectations for our team members. Maintaining accountability, consistently and across the board, around the behaviors that model those values is an absolute necessity for ever sustaining those expectations. But accountability isn't directly synonymous with formal disciplinary action. At least, it shouldn't be...

> **Maintaining accountability,
> consistently and across the board,
> around the behaviors that model those values
> is an absolute necessity for ever sustaining
> those expectations.**

Several years ago, while talking with the owner of a company, one of his supervisors came by his office in a lather about a relatively new employee. The supervisor's first words were: "I can't believe you haven't fired that clown yet!" The owner was caught off guard. He'd spoken with the supervisor about that employee's progress at least once a week over the month and a half since they were hired. I know that for a fact, because I was involved in most of those conversations. Each time, the supervisor was at least mildly pleased, if not glowing, in his feedback.

As we worked to determine what had moved the needle so far so quickly, we learned that there had indeed been several minor issues all along—but the supervisor didn't feel that any of those issues were worth the time it would take to address. Unfortunately, not addressing those relatively minor missteps led to a precipitous drop-off in the new employee's adherence to expectations. It was a quintessential case of "give 'em an inch, and they'll take a mile." That supervisor (like so many others I've seen over the years) went from mildly annoyed to full-on pissed off overnight—or at least that's how it came across to me and the owner of the company.

Had I been the HR Manager for that company, I could have worked with the supervisor and owner to begin documenting the specific issues, as well as addressing each according to the organization's detailed progressive disciplinary process. Even then, though, we wouldn't have moved straight to "firing that clown" like the supervisor wanted. Whether we're addressing behavior that clearly violates company policy, or dealing with a situation where a team member has just fallen short of one of our core values, a one-on-one conversation is nearly always the best place to start.

Yes, there are exceptions; some policy violations lead directly to termination—do not pass go, do not collect $200. The same holds true when it comes to our values. But for the most part, our role as leaders should be to guide behavior toward those high (yet sustainable) expectations we've set, rather than actively looking for ways to condemn someone for failing to meet them. Many times, when that new(er) team member isn't meeting expectations, it's because we haven't provided them with the support necessary to do so.

Regardless of the issue, a direct (yet kind) conversation about what missed the mark and how we expect them to change their behavior to meet and exceed our expectations can become a valuable training opportunity. All too often, these are entirely missed because "we just don't have time" to deal with the issue at the moment, and frustration builds gradually until we finally reach a boiling point. In *What's KILLING Your Profitability?*, I dedicated two whole chapters to the costs businesses deal with daily, from high turnover and poor recruiting—which are often lumped together but are truly separate issues that feed each other.

For our purposes here, know it costs far too much to get and keep good people to shirk our leadership responsibility by failing to hold them accountable early on, which tells them we're actually okay with the poor behavior, then pushing them out the door when we've had all we can stand.

That's not leadership! When we address any misstep by detailing how it doesn't align with our values, and detailing what they can do instead to exemplify those values, we create a culture of accountability rather than one of condemnation. As we do this routinely, we have a chance to help our team members build habits around our company values. Let's look at some simple steps for that.

Accountability Builds Habits

From nearly the beginning of this book, I've stressed the critical role habits play in everything we do. I introduced the idea of helping our team members connect their behavior to core company values by sharing that it would require a slight change in our approach, and how that would allow them to repeat the necessary actions long enough to establish habits. I hit on it heavily again when we examined how building strong habits gives us the bandwidth to make changes on the fly as we deal with unexpected issues, even when the initial process isn't particularly exciting on any given day.

Before we wrap up this look at how sustaining high expectations around our values truly allows our organizations to create a lasting legacy, let's make sure we have simple steps in place to develop the kind of accountability that can indeed establish the proper habits.

I'll stress once more that holding our teams accountable is far more about coaching them toward the desired behavior than condemning them for stepping out of line ever so slightly. When we take advantage of every opportunity to shine a positive light on the behaviors, addressing any behavior that doesn't align with a core value becomes much more natural. In either case, however, we must be incredibly specific about how their behavior relates to or does not relate to the value in question. If we only discuss our values with them when something goes wrong, they're unlikely to have a clear picture of what the desired behavior looks like.

As a result, we'll be reinforcing the undesired action as the actual outcome moving forward. Remember, recognized behavior gets repeated. When we're intentional about recognizing the routine ways our team members' behavior models our core values, even when that's through a quick and simple pat on their back in a one-on-one interaction, we're providing them with feedback that establishes accountability, and helps build those ever-so-important habits that make our highest expectations sustainable.

> **Providing them with feedback that establishes accountability, and helps build those ever-so-important habits that make our highest expectations sustainable.**

To prove that I still live in reality, let's address the remaining elephant in the room: what about the times when someone just won't align with our values? Make no mistake, I've seen a positive coaching approach produce far better results than a strictly punitive approach. However, there will still be times when we need to take formal disciplinary action into account to have any hope of holding our teams accountable. Someone, at some point, will feel compelled to test any boundary we've worked to establish. When their actions go against our core values, we have no choice but to act on the decisions they've made.

In most cases, we'll still address whatever they've done through an initial conversation. However, if they choose to continue using the same unacceptable behaviors afterward, they're effectively demanding that we walk them through our formal progressive disciplinary process, up to and including termination. The latter, of course, is never something I've enjoyed doing. Truth be told, the only way I was able to get comfortable with having these conversations was by realizing that it was truly their choice, not mine.

While it's not a step any leader ever looks forward to, it's a crucial part of building and maintaining accountability with the individual who has stepped out of line, as well as with every team member who has worked to meet or exceed what we expect in modeling our values. In cases where a team member refuses to align with our core values, they're effectively telling us they no longer want to be part of our organization. While it's certainly difficult for us to address at that moment, we need to be accountable to everyone else on our teams as we uphold those core values. When we've established simple practices for exemplifying our core values and consistently explained and recognized behaviors that align with them, we're well on our way to helping establish habits throughout our teams that sustain our high expectations. Over time, this is exactly what will produce the results we're working toward.

Sustaining High Expectations Around Our Values

Setting high expectations for modeling our core company values is a must. That said, getting our teams to perform at that level, on a routine basis, will only happen if we're willing to establish a culture of accountability. I'm not suggesting this is based solely on enforcing discipline, rather on creating an atmosphere where each team member knows exactly what's expected of them, why it matters, and the specific ramifications of their actions in exemplifying our values, as well as when they fall short of the mark. Without that kind of accountability in place, any time we rant about the importance of our values will eventually be viewed as empty talk.

While most of what I shared just before this was focused on helping individuals on our teams create habits that build our values into their daily tasks, each thing they do personally contributes directly to the results our organization achieves as a whole. Establishing accountability with each team member, from the newest, least experienced to the most senior and highly skilled, not only sets the tone for the results they achieve in their own role but also does so much more—that's how our internal culture builds around what we've defined as our core values.

If Truett Cathy had backed off his insistence on saying "My Pleasure" with his most tenured drink-filler-upper, what message would he have sent to the trainees? And what if Craig allowed his son to be rude to their team members or customers? Would others around them have bought into any of their core values, let alone *family*?

When we, as leaders, are willing to develop the discipline within ourselves to establish and maintain accountability for living out our values in every role within our company, we can transform the actions of each team member into an internal culture that perpetuates itself. That said, failing to discipline ourselves in this way has a perpetuating effect on our culture, too—just not in a way we'll be very excited to accept responsibility for, and it usually happens much quicker.

When we can establish accountability around our values and do it consistently for a long enough period, we'll begin to see it take root within our culture. We'll then be well on our way to building a strong external reputation that our organization is known for far and wide. And since this never happens as quickly as we'd like, our efforts to keep the importance of each value in front of our teams will need to be ongoing, and we'll need to help them develop a clear picture of the legacy we're working toward.

Casting a Vision, Built on Our Values

To sustain the effort required by our high expectations, accountability must be built into our culture—at all levels. However, detailing what our team members need to do, and how that needs to happen, is only part of that process. Even the most ingrained habits supporting the simplest behaviors can still be incredibly tough to maintain when things go awry. Our best shot at providing our team members with the inspiration they need for consistently choosing the harder right over the easier wrong won't come from understanding exactly *what* our core values mean, or precisely *how* they should be modeling those values in their daily routine. This will require us to help them see exactly *why* living out each value matters every single day. We'll need to become experts at casting a vision that's built on our values.

> **Even the most ingrained habits supporting the simplest behaviors can still be incredibly tough to maintain when things go awry.**

I opened *Leading With A Clear Purpose* by emphasizing just how daunting leadership can be without a particular reason—a clear purpose, if you will—for accepting the challenges of leading rather than simply going through the motions in a typical job. The second half of the book built on that idea, challenging leaders to provide that same type of clear purpose for each of their team members. Not only does that help each of us fight off the increasingly prevalent risk of burnout, but a clear and definite purpose can be the driving force that earns the 57% increase in discretionary effort I referenced multiple times in that book, and almost constantly throughout *What's KILLING Your Profitability?*...

For even the best team members, or leaders, to consistently put in the effort of exemplifying our core values, connecting *what* those values mean and *how* we each display them in practice, casting a vision that details how achieving our organizational purpose is achieved, and who we impact in the process, truly serves as that critical *why*—for our team members and ourselves!

In 2017, a friend provided the opening keynote for an event Cindy and I hosted. He shared a message detailing the legacy his late wife built for their family through her battle with breast cancer. Thankfully, only a select few in the audience could relate to what he and his children experienced. Still, he was very intentional about tying that message back to challenging everyone to identify the legacy they wanted to leave. When we paint a picture of the clear purpose our organization is working to achieve, in a way that everyone on our team can connect with, we'll have the foundation for creating a legacy built on our core company values.

This should never be focused solely on reaching our own goals or the company's objectives; it should also be geared toward helping everyone involved win.

Values that Ensure Everyone Wins

In the final lesson of our *Emerging Leader Development* course, Cindy opens by challenging participants to consider the real driver behind why they've accepted leadership responsibility. She goes on to compare things like power, position, money, and prestige with influence, growth, opportunities, and serving others. The first batch is tied directly to the individual and the second on the teams led by those individuals. Whether we like it or not, our team members depend on us.

Along those same lines, I recently had a conversation with a friend who heads a state agency dedicated to serving veterans with barriers to employment. He shared a scenario he had just been through, where a comment he made in jest to a coworker he had always interacted well with was received far differently than he ever imagined. Rather than in the spirit of camaraderie he intended, the coworker verbally attacked him, saying that his comment was offensive. He asked if I had experienced anything like this, where someone seemed to be looking for something to be offended by.

I explained two separate scenarios. The first: during a small group session that Cindy and I facilitated soon after starting our business, one of the participants repeatedly asked what would keep someone from using the concepts to manipulate others. After attempting to address their concern kindly several times, my patience wore thin, and I drew a line in the sand by stating, "The only way I know to avoid being manipulative is not to be manipulative!" In case you're wondering, that didn't please the participant, but the question didn't come up again.

The second scenario involved a business owner who was constantly suspicious of how any service provider he dealt with was trying to "get one over on him." While I've enjoyed most of the interaction I had with him over the years, I could never understand why he put so much thought into that. There are indeed shady characters out there, but those are generally few and far between, and their shenanigans usually stand out like a sore thumb. I realized over time that, although pleasant one-on-one, he was often looking for an angle to take advantage of most of the people he dealt with, including his team members.

Discussing both scenarios with my friend, I explained that, at least in my experience, individuals who looked for negativity in others were often the ones dishing out that same treatment and, therefore, expected it from anyone they dealt with.

When casting our vision of the legacy we hope to achieve by living out our core values, simple practices are essential. We also need to hold everyone involved accountable to our high expectations. Our consistent example is critical, and that example must be one that clearly demonstrates how modeling our company values serves everyone in the equation: the clients & community we serve, everyone on our team, and lastly, ourselves. When everyone we serve wins, we have a real chance of creating a lasting legacy based on those values—and achieving our organizational purpose.

> **That example must be one that clearly demonstrates how modeling our company values serves everyone in the equation.**

With all this in place, we'll wrap things up soon by working through some real-life examples with hopes of providing some clarity of what to do—as well as some pitfalls to avoid along the way.

CHAPTER TEN

THE IMPACT OF OUR CORE VALUES: GOOD AND BAD

Now we have an outline in place for basing our organization's foundation on core values—the simple practices we'll need to provide for acting on those values, the consistent example we'll need to be in living them out, and the sustainable expectation for how our values are part of everything each team member does daily.

Let's look at how much impact these things can have. I'll start by sharing an example of what can happen when core values aren't clearly communicated internally, or even worse, anything remotely resembling stated values ends up being empty words that are routinely violated by the organization's executive team. After that, I'll provide several examples of companies that Cindy and I've observed firsthand as they've built strong cultures around their core values. Then, before tying this all together with a simple framework for creating a great culture around *your* core company values, I'll challenge you with something you should consider every single day you carry the responsibility of leading a team.

Make no mistake, though, I'm certainly not suggesting that any of this will ever be easy. Regardless of how big (or small) your organization is today, building specific values into everything you do will require tremendous and constant focus. Depending on where you are, and how much you've discussed your values with your existing team, this may initially be an uphill battle. That said, the juice will definitely be worth the squeeze. I mean, what's the alternative? Forever struggling in every aspect of our business simply because we weren't willing to develop the self-discipline to identify and live out a set of values? That sounds miserable to me, and I'm guessing it does to you as well.

For anything we've worked through to this point, or the simple framework we'll close with to have any lasting impact, there are a few things that must happen. We'll need to develop a realistic picture of exactly where we are currently. This isn't always enjoyable, and will require receiving the feedback we need to hear rather than just the input that feels good. We'll also need to accept the responsibility for driving any changes that need to be made. No one is coming to our rescue. And we'll need to fight the urge to justify not taking action.

There are just as many excuses for a large company to stick with the status quo as there are for a small one. Don't fall into that trap! Large organizations tend to have more resources available, specifically in terms of personnel and finances, but that generally means there are a lot more team members we need to reach with our message, and to help change their behaviors. Smaller companies are often nimbler, but they usually have every team member spinning multiple plates, even before attempting the slightest change.

I've often heard the adage that the best time to plant a shade tree was twenty years ago, and the second best time is right now. We can't change anything we've done—or haven't done—up to this point. If you're happy with where you are today, great! Let's build on that. If you already see opportunities for improvement, there's no better time than now to start the process.

With all that in mind, let's look at a bit of a cautionary tale.

Losing Ground Without Core Values

Earlier, when we examined how to rally our team around our core values, I briefly mentioned a longstanding organization that once had world-class talent leading each separate department, but had experienced significant turnover in critical roles. While some of this was due to planned retirements, the majority wasn't. The individuals who didn't retire either went to work for competitors, or started their own businesses, actively competing against their former employer.

While doing research for our *Recruitment, Retention, & Culture* course, designed to provide leaders with a guide for building a great team rather than something explicitly geared at the Human Resources community, I found a statistic from the Bureau of Labor Statistics showing that the average voluntary turnover rate nationwide, across all industries, was just shy of twenty-five percent annually. (I referenced this earlier in detailing how impressive it was to see the company Craig & Kim bought have only five percent turnover after twenty-four months.)

Throughout my three and a half decades in the workforce, I've observed that the most significant portion of voluntary turnover has been among employees who have been with a company for less than five years, with a substantial portion comprising individuals with under two years of service. There are numerous reasons for this, but nearly all of them tie back to them not being given a solid reason to stay. The culture wasn't something they bought into. They hadn't connected with the company's core values.

In contrast, the company I alluded to earlier has experienced turnover in almost all its critical roles in less than a decade—and some of those positions have been filled multiple times. While two of these were planned retirements, the rest were not. Of those who didn't retire, at least six new small businesses now exist in the same area, all serving the same customer base. Additionally, I'm aware of at least a dozen highly skilled and motivated employees who now receive their W2 from a competitor. There were a few other retirements in the mix, but at least one of those was almost a decade early, and mainly because he no longer felt like he had something to strive for: what he valued, and what the company he had served for so long valued, were no longer aligned.

Interestingly enough, nothing in that organization changed overnight. If anything, change took far too long, and rarely had the teeth to make a positive impact or be sustained over time. And since the company had developed a solid reputation (and balance sheet) over many preceding decades, the folks who had the final say on critical decisions seemed to be more tuned in with how great things had been than where they were at present. Now, let's look at how quickly that slope became slippery.

The People Involved Will Change, The Values Can't

Turnover is always going to happen. Part of leading responsibly is to plan for that. And in preparing for each type of inevitable turnover—a retirement, a termination due to unacceptable performance, or someone leaving for a competitor or to join one—our core company values must remain unchanged. While the organization I'm referencing didn't abruptly abandon a set of longstanding values that had been in place and discussed openly for generations, small changes (that every business faces) were occurring routinely, and had a compounding effect over time.

I remember being awestruck when I got a firsthand glimpse of the caliber of people heading up each part of this small-to-midsize business; I had seen organizations four and five times their size, with just a fraction of the talent and expertise in each business unit. The most interesting aspect? None of those individuals were nearing the end of their careers, despite having each been with the company, or at least in that specific industry, for more than a decade. The boss was relatively soft-spoken and an absolute master of the craft on which the organization had been built.

However, like many of the more reserved individuals in leadership roles, he didn't enjoy conflict and cared deeply about his long-tenured team. So he rarely addressed performance that fell short of the values he and the most senior employees held dear. Since the majority of the team was exceptionally skilled at what they did, though, fortunately such tough conversations were rare. The rest of the team essentially policed the few individuals who were willing to push the boundaries, but even those few were highly skilled in their roles.

Like all companies, though, a succession plan was necessary and was being implemented. Even in the best scenarios, a new boss won't have the same expertise right away, and will have to earn the team's trust and buy-in. Both require time and an incredible amount of intentional effort; neither happens automatically. If the person taking the reins isn't willing to develop strong relationships with the key players on the team around them, they often end up getting only the feedback they want to hear, rather than what they need to hear in order to grow into their role and earn the respect necessary to truly lead. And if relationships are never built, top performers will not stick around. The best people in any industry can make a great living almost anywhere they want; the core values of the organization are often exactly why they stay or go.

> **The best people in any industry can make a great living almost anywhere they want; the core values of the organization are often exactly why they stay or go.**

Although not all at once, a few of the long-tenured and highly skilled team members did move on. Replacing their talent was difficult enough, but replacing it with people who would be as loyal was just not possible. This led to an almost immediate drop in how value-straying employees were held accountable. Since several team members who had previously done this had moved on, the bosses were the only ones left to do it. The one who had earned respect over the years was a bit reluctant, and the one who hadn't earned respect was far too willing, and you can guess how well that was received.

As the slope became increasingly slippery, a few other key players also left. Of those who had left, one started a small business in direct competition with them. As the more established company's culture drifted away from the values once held so dear, several highly skilled team members moved to the new company—mainly because the owner had earned their respect by upholding his core values.

You can look in any direction today and find an article detailing the woes of attracting top talent in any field. As this issue has become more prevalent, and as those with the most in-demand skills have become able to name their price, a primary separator between the company that throws bags of money to attract a candidate and one that has great team members asking to join the team, will be how the organization's foundation has been built on core values, how expectations for modeling those values have been communicated internally and externally, and how everyone involved is held accountable to those values—by the leadership team initially, and eventually by each other.

With this example in mind, let's examine how a few companies with cultures built on strong values have attracted top talent (and great clients) instead of creating their own competition.

Compounding Success Around Core Values

In *The 21 Irrefutable Laws of Leadership*[36], John Maxwell explains The Law of the Mirror by simply saying, "We attract who we are, not who we want." I had never seen a more obvious example than the organization I just referenced, initially as I became familiar with the company and even more so as the succession process unfolded. Before the changes, the team consisted of the most talented group I had ever seen in one place, and that was even more impressive given the area they were in and the total headcount.

Like the fellow calling the shots, each of them was extremely detail-oriented and relatively reserved in their approach. But as he handed off more and more control to his successor, who cared far less about the details involved and was much more deliberate in his approach, the team that took shape around him soon shared those attributes. Had the new look of the team maintained the organization's founding values, sustainable growth wouldn't have been an issue; that wasn't the case.

Even the most tenured, skilled, and loyal team members will eventually move on when the core values displayed by those in leadership roles no longer match their own. A company with leaders who vehemently protect the culture they've built, as well as the values it's built on, will not only be one where the best team members stay indefinitely, it will (at least eventually) attract a constant flow of great people who want to join the team.

**A company with leaders who vehemently protect the culture they've built, as well as the values it's built on, will not only be one where the best team members stay indefinitely,
it will (at least eventually) attract a constant flow of great people who want to join the team.**

Don't misunderstand me here. This will never just happen, and it will not be easy to achieve, but replacing top talent without a foundation built around your core values is far more difficult.

At this point in my career, I've had the privilege of witnessing leaders build outstanding teams around their closely held core values in both large and small companies, in the workplace, and volunteer organizations across every sector of society. The type of work, the level of compensation, and even the pedigree of the individual leading the team have had far less to do with earning commitment from those involved than how those leaders modeled their core values.

To drive this point home, I'll detail some of the best examples I've had direct experience with. In each case, these leaders could have made an occasional compromise to increase their team's overall capacity, and achieve greater profitability in the short term. However, by having the discipline to stand by what they've valued most, I've watched each of their organizations steadily grow, attracting some of the best people in their respective industries.

Real-Life Examples of Building Around Core Values

While under what was likely the most intense pressure I'd ever experienced to fill open positions, one of the managers I was supporting informed me that, by the following week, he needed seven people with a particular skill set.

It just so happened that I had all the applications for that position in my hand as we spoke. I explained that, of the five we had, two were more suited for a restraining order than a job offer, one had no relevant experience, and the remaining two were probably worth interviewing. I handed him the applications and told him to let me know which seven (of those five) he had the most interest in adding to his team. He replied, "Just do the best you can," and walked away.

Regardless of industry, current economic climate, or pressing business demands, I've rarely seen a time when any organization has too many talented team members living out their core values. What I have seen far too often is a compromise on upholding those values, even if only slightly, resulting in questionable hiring decisions that negatively impact the organization's culture. However, I've had the privilege of seeing the inverse as well.

> **A compromise on upholding those values, even if only slightly, resulting in questionable hiring decisions that negatively impact the organization's culture.**

Over the last decade or so, I've worked with several leaders who were adamant about only adding team members who matched their core company values rather than filling a spot on their roster with whoever had the basic skills for the open position. I won't pretend it was ever easy for them. In fact, it was nearly every time harder at the moment. But if you remember what I learned from Terry about choosing the harder right over the easier wrong, you can guess where I'm going with this...

Several years ago, I had a scheduled lunch meeting with a friend just after he was supposed to have selected a candidate for a key role on his team. He had accepted a promotion from Deputy Chief to Chief in a reasonably large city's Fire Department, and he was working to backfill the position he had been in. He and his team had interviewed several candidates with all the necessary skills to excel in the role, but none could explain why they were interested in joining this specific team; none were a direct match for what that team valued most.

Since my friend had been juggling the duties of both roles for several months, it would have been so much easier at the time to select the best of that batch and move on. They did not. He and his team opted to post the position again rather than settle. That decision yielded a great person for the role, one who has truly embodied the organization's core values from the outset, and has continued to do so ever since.

Another example is a close friend who acquired his company in 2016. I helped with the majority of his staffing from late 2017 until early 2022. Throughout that time, he always had positions to fill, a few due to regular turnover, but mostly because they consistently generated new opportunities. I can point to dozens of conversations during that time where he was satisfied that the candidate could do the work, but was unsure whether the candidate would be a good match for the values on which he was building the company. As I write this, that organization has experienced 5X growth since he took over, and is currently on pace to double year over year.

Two other examples are businesses that offer very specific services in their respective markets. The leaders of each maintain incredibly high expectations of their team members, and they base those expectations around the core values they detail routinely. While operating in very different industries, both companies have earned outstanding reputations among the clients they serve, as well as within the communities in which they operate. If you're ever in their area(s) and need what either business offers, I'm confident you'd receive a referral to both from nearly anyone you ask. All that stems from how those teams embody their core values.

Since I've already referenced numerous examples from the businesses Craig and Kim operate, I'll skip them here. But I could go on and on about the growth I've seen their team experience, and how their core values have been the foundation for it all.

The last example I'll share is of a friend in a leadership role in law enforcement. He took a new position in early 2022. Like many organizations where a new leader takes over, he saw nearly thirty percent turnover in just the first few months. That said, turnover ain't always bad. Those who chose to leave so quickly were quite accustomed to doing the bare minimum, and my friend's expectation of exemplifying the department's core values and providing a premium level of service to their community wasn't something they were willing to live up to. Since then, he has developed a reputation among the citizens, business owners, and elected officials in his area that I've never seen.

Each of these leaders has played a crucial role in helping their organizations establish a strong reputation in their respective areas and industries. Interestingly enough, more than half of them are also experiencing something few organizations ever do: having a waiting list of individuals who want to join their teams. And the ones that don't (yet) are moving in that direction rapidly. None of this happens without a solid foundation built on core values.

Let's examine why this happens before exploring exactly how we can do it with the teams we lead.

A Values-Based Culture Attracts Great People

In *The 15 Invaluable Laws of Growth*[37], John Maxwell emphasizes that "growth compounds and accelerates *if* we remain intentional about it." Compounding interest in growth or our finances can work for or against us. If you're not entirely sure this is true, have your banker run some numbers to show what happens to a high credit card balance when making only the minimum payment, compared to how a retirement plan can grow over time with the same amount added each month.

The same holds true for our organizational culture, which is built around a core set of values. These values may be the ones listed in our handbooks and displayed on our walls, or they may be a wildly different set of values that we show our teams, contrary to what's in print. While the folks running one company didn't set out to openly violate the core values it had been built on, gradual moves away from those values had a compounding impact that resulted in costly turnover.

> **Gradual moves away from those values**
> **had a compounding impact**
> **that resulted in costly turnover.**

In each organization, I observed where leaders stood firm by what they valued most, even when a compromise here or there would have made life easier presently for them. I also saw a compounding impact. Like compounding interest, the direction depends on our actions.

In both *What's KILLING Your Profitability?* and *Leading With A Clear Purpose*, I provided examples detailing how top-tier individuals in any industry do not jump ship just because things get difficult. If anything, challenges bring out the best in them and our team as a whole—as long as expectations are high, everyone is held to the same level of accountability, and we uphold our clearly stated core values at all costs. Failing to do these things may not immediately result in everyone leaving at once, but you can bet the team members who strive for excellence won't be around long. There's a chance that an organization without a strong value-foundation can attract a rockstar occasionally; even a broken clock is right twice a day. (You won't get that reference if you've only ever used digital clocks...).

The good news? Not only will consistently working to solidifying core values bring out the best in our amazing team members, it will, sooner or later, yield a culture that even great people outside our organization hear about and want to join. The best people I've ever been around have had one thing in common: they want to be part of a winning team. In fact, I've met very few who don't.

Before mapping out a simple yet specific framework for building your foundation around a clear set of core values, let's examine what we absolutely must do as leaders to ensure that this compounding effect is working for us rather than against us.

Great Programs are Built on Strong Values

Building a thriving, self-perpetuating, values-based culture will indeed produce wins for everyone involved, but winning won't be the sole motivation for the great people we attract to our team through this process. High standards, consistently exceeding expectations, and an atmosphere of genuine accountability will be just as important. While I've never followed college or professional sports all that closely—with one exception I'll get to shortly—I have studied several legendary coaches, not just because of the results their teams achieved, but more to learn why they consistently attracted outstanding talent *and* how they were able to get those all-star athletes to form a cohesive team.

> **High standards, consistently exceeding expectations, and an atmosphere of genuine accountability will be just as important.**

In the spring of 2001, I had the opportunity to hear Lou Holtz speak. Coincidentally, that was part of the same event where I heard John Maxwell speak for the first time—just weeks after initially reading *The 21 Irrefutable Laws of Leadership*. Holtz shared some hilarious stories, but the one that stood out most was about benching two Notre Dame players just before the team's appearance in the Orange Bowl. These weren't just any players; they were responsible for over fifty percent of the scoring throughout the season.

It wasn't his choice, he explained. It was theirs. He had set a curfew for team members the night before each game. All season long, players were expected to be in by a given time, or they'd sit out the first half of the game. Those two players chose to violate that curfew the night before their biggest game of the year. I won't share his entire story here, but the team won the game mainly because Holtz had built a team around a set of core values rather than around any individual players. In a recent lesson Cindy and I shared with a group, I quoted Holtz as saying, "I've coached good players, and I've coached bad players. I'm a better coach with good players." As true as that may be, those good players only have a chance to reach their full potential when foundational values are in place.

> **Good players only have a chance to reach their full potential when foundational values are in place.**

Another excellent coach I've studied is Joe Gibbs. Interestingly enough, I heard him speak at an event with Maxwell one year after hearing Lou Holtz. Gibbs is the only person that I'm aware of who has led teams to championships in two different professional sports; the Washington Redskins in football and Tony Stewart's Home Depot team in NASCAR. He shared some incredible insight in that 2002 session, but the most memorable lesson was from his book, *Racing to Win*[38].

If you know anything about Tony Stewart, you know he developed quite a reputation for being a hothead. Hell, that's why I liked him! In the book, Gibbs shared how he finally had to address it. Tony was winning races and racking up points, but his temper was not exemplifying the values that Gibbs and Home Depot were willing to build around. He sat Stewart down and explained the changes they expected and the path he'd find himself on if he chose not to make those changes. Their championship came after that conversation.

Yet another example is Mike Krzyzewski, also known as Coach K, longtime head coach at Duke. Long before the destruction of college sports we've seen unfold due to the NIL model, Coach K routinely attracted top-tier high school talent every year. While his teams consistently had winning records, I'm convinced that this wasn't the primary driver, given they won just five NCAA championships over 42 years, with only two of those being back-to-back. Based on my research into his books and conversations with someone I knew who was close to him at the time, those who came to play for him did so because he earned a reputation for bringing out the best in each of them and building strong teams. He worked those teams *hard*, all around a set of core values.

For one final sports analogy, let's consider the Boston Red Sox, the only team I've ever followed closely over the years. As a kid, they were my absolute favorite team, of any sport. I mentioned earlier that everyone "wants to be part of a winning team," but that wasn't what drew me to the pre-2004 Red Sox. I opened part two of *Leading With A Clear Purpose* with a chapter titled "It Ain't (Just) About the Pay, Purpose Matters!" The same holds true for values and accountability. What I loved about those Red Sox, even as perennial losers (86 years without winning a World Series), was the underdog spirit and their constant grit against the hated New York Yankees.

That said, I remember precisely when I stopped following them closely. Although I had always respected Terry Francona as a manager and admired him for leading the team to World Series wins in 2004 and 2007, he failed to maintain accountability with the team through the second half of the 2011 season, and I've paid little attention to them as an organization since. I distinctly remember them losing 20 games in the last month of that season and missing the playoffs, all while star pitchers John Lackey (who I never really cared for) and Josh Beckett were weathering accusations of drinking beer and eating fried chicken in the dugout during games. They denied it, but something was clearly amiss for a team with so much talent to drop off so drastically, so fast. It pushed me away, but it also cost the team a spot in the postseason.

As with each of these examples, how our organizations are built really does depend on what we do as leaders to embed our core values. With high expectations and consistent accountability, we can attract great people and build strong teams. Without that, even our solid team members can slip through our hands. It all rests on whether we're willing to take responsibility for upholding those core organizational values.

Values, Good or Bad, Tie Back to Leadership

While Terry Francona was the manager of the Boston Red Sox during 2011's late-season collapse, and his contract option wasn't renewed afterward, I'm not placing the blame solely on him. Quite frankly, I thought John Lackey was a goon long before that. While Francona held the "manager" title, there are numerous people within every professional baseball organization who have as much or more control over the purse strings, and who play a significant role in shaping the team's culture. That said, we rarely know the names of those others, nor are they usually the ones moving to a new city and team after such a debacle. The manager, or whatever the position is called in a given sport, is the public-facing *leader* in the organization.

One of the first (and oft-repeated) catchphrases I remember hearing from John Maxwell was, "Everything rises and falls on leadership." Through all that, one specific story stands out. John was sharing an interaction he had with a venture capital group that had a long history of purchasing struggling businesses, turning those businesses around, then selling them at a substantial profit. He asked one of them if there were any specific things they did with every business, regardless of industry. They immediately responded that the first thing that's done in every acquisition is to get rid of the existing executive team.

John pushed back, asking if it was necessary *every time*. The group members were adamant that this was critical. If those executives had been effective in their roles, the company wouldn't have been struggling, and wouldn't have been in a position for this venture capital group to buy them out.

That example solidified John's statement for me: *everything truly does rise and fall on leadership*. While Francona's tenure in Boston ended after closing the 2011 season with a 7-20 September record, his role as a leader did not. He became the manager of the Cleveland Indians in 2013 and was named American League Manager of the Year that same year. He earned that designation two more times during his stint with the Indians/Guardians organization.

I've never met Terry Francona, but what he's achieved since that 2011 Red Sox meltdown tells me he shares one particular trait with the most effective leaders I've ever known: he took responsibility for what happened around him and made changes. Although I am not aware of the specific changes Francona made, the results he achieved in Cleveland speak for themselves.

That said, I have had the opportunity to work directly with numerous other leaders as they've encountered challenges. The common thread has been that, regardless of which individual on their respective teams dropped the ball that initially created the issue, these leaders have been willing to accept personal responsibility rather than blaming a team member.

Since I've referenced Craig so many times to this point, I'll start with him. He and I have worked through several scenarios where clients came to him with complaints. Every single time, I've seen Craig take responsibility and work to find a solution. The friend I mentioned before, who's experienced 5X growth in less than a decade since purchasing his business, used to have a sign on his desk that read "The Buck Stops Here," not out of the kind of arrogance to imply he had the last say, but to send the message to anyone coming to him that he's always willing to help with an issue.

In looking at how this applies to our core organizational values, John's statement is spot on: "Everything rises and falls on leadership."

If the culture does not attract and retain great people, that's on us as leaders. If we're blessed with a consistent stream of exceptional candidates reaching out to join our team, that ties back to how we've instilled those values into the organizations we lead. But we can't afford to take our foot off the gas!

With that in mind, let's consider just how frequently we need to put our values in front of our team members.

Good Intentions Are Never Enough

I'll quote John once more to make sure it sinks in: "Everything rises and falls on leadership." If as leaders we're not excited about how our core values are currently serving as the foundation of our organization, that's on us. If we're happy with that foundation, keep up the good work—and be sure to acknowledge everyone on the team who has played a role in consistently modeling those values to get to this point.

The best leaders I've ever had the privilege of working with have been quick to accept responsibility for missteps and even quicker to share the credit for success. All in all, I've seen some truly exceptional individuals in leadership roles who have had the best of intentions, but who still fell short of establishing a strong foundation around the values they held most dear. Good intentions are *never* enough!

> **I've seen some truly exceptional individuals in leadership roles who have had the best of intentions, but who still fell short of establishing a strong foundation around the values they held most dear.**

Through this process, I've provided multiple examples detailing how some of our closest friends and most cherished clients have instilled their core organizational values into the culture of the teams they lead. None of that has happened by accident; all of them have been diligent in talking about and exemplifying their values daily. And this hasn't been something they were able to do for a short period before it took hold; it often takes years to develop. For perspective, I'll emphasize once more that it took Truett Cathy [39]ten years to embed the "My Pleasure" that you and I expect to hear multiple times in any Chick-fil-A we may visit.

Cindy and I had two separate conversations recently where we've stressed exactly this, both with outstanding folks leading strong teams. In our last session with the executive team we're supporting, we discussed extensively the importance of ensuring that every single member of their respective teams was crystal clear on the impact their organization strives to achieve with each client they serve. One of the senior members of the group asked if it was possible to talk about their organization's purpose too often. I was adamant that there's no such thing as "too often" when our purpose is meaningful. The same holds true for weaving our values into conversations with our teams. When those values matter—and I can't think of a situation where they wouldn't—there's no such thing as too much.

In the second conversation, a key leader in an organization we work with shared what he perceived as resistance to the organizational purpose he began detailing with his team. As we discussed this with him, it sounded more as though these team members were processing the idea rather than pushing back on it. We encouraged him to stay the course, to be sure to include the impact they're having on everyone they serve in each conversation he has with his team, collectively and individually.

Much like many great people we've worked with over the years, both of these leaders cared deeply about each member of their teams. Neither wanted to come across as sharing a canned message or being redundant. All too often, we understand the message we've shared with our team and assume they've received it just as we expressed it. We have the best of intentions, aiming to make a positive impact on everyone involved without coming across as too pushy. But even with the best intentions, we can fall far short of our goal. Having a framework for explicitly, consistently detailing our values is crucial to building them into the foundation of our organization. To wrap up this entire process, we'll work through a simple and strategic process for leading from a foundation of clearly defined core values.

SECTION THREE

A FRAMEWORK FOR LASTING IMPACT

Chapter 11 distills the book's insights into a simple, actionable framework for building a values-driven organization. Using three strategic questions—*What do you want to be known for? What are you known for? Do they match?*—this section guides leaders to define, align, and embed core values with consistency and accountability. Drawing on the IMPACT acronym listing Dove Development & Consulting's values, and client examples, it emphasizes intentional communication and visible modeling to create lasting impact.

CHAPTER ELEVEN

A FRAMEWORK FOR DEFINING YOUR CORE VALUES; THE ONES YOU'RE KNOWN FOR

While the best organizations I've ever had the pleasure of working with, or studying, are indeed built on the foundation of strong values, it never happens by chance. Even the best of intentions won't yield the lasting results we're capable of achieving when we develop the discipline of adhering to a simple framework. And that framework needs to be one for defining the values we want our organizations to be known *FOR*...

For several years, Cindy and I served on a "President's Advisory Council" for Maxwell Leadership. Throughout most of that time, our role was to support individuals worldwide in hosting their local Live2Lead events. Volunteering in that capacity helped us develop a closer relationship with Mark Cole, who wrote the foreword for *What's KILLING Your Profitability? (It ALL Boils Down to Leadership!)* and served as our closing keynote speaker at The 2025 LeadershipLegacy Experience, but we also got to know a fellow named Jeff Henderson[40]. I referenced the initial call where we first met Jeff, as I challenged you to consider *'Who Really Cares About Your Values?'* and I shared the three powerful questions that Jeff posed for each of us during that call. With all we've covered to this point, now is where those questions matter most. The framework we're about to work through will be incredibly simple; a bunch of pomp and circumstance just won't stick. However, if we're not willing to be completely transparent in how we answer each of those questions, we'll be kidding ourselves, and doing a disservice to every team member who counts on us for leadership.

As a quick reminder, here are the questions again:

1. What DO YOU WANT to be known for?
2. What ARE YOU known for?
3. Do they match?

Asking ourselves these three basic questions is easy enough. Answering them honestly, especially if we're not happy with our answers, takes quite a bit of courage—at least it did for us!

I've studied leadership, communication, and human behavior more in my life than any other topics. Cindy and I have worked closely with some amazing leaders and their entire organizations as we've pursued what we now list as our mission statement: "Improving Your Profitability by Building Better Leaders." Throughout all of this, we've spoken with leaders across the United States about the importance of ensuring each individual on their team has complete clarity about how the work they're responsible for ties back to their organization's mission, vision, and values.

While many of them achieved solid results, we realized we were, essentially, shoeless cobblers. Although Cindy and I shared some deeply held values that have helped us build a strong marriage and business partnership, we hadn't taken the time to put them in writing for anyone to see. To achieve the **IMPACT** we truly wanted to make, we needed to lead by example in this area as much as in any other. So here are the cobblers' shoes:

- *Intentionality* - We are intentional in everything we do, ensuring we make a positive difference daily;
- *Measurability* - Measuring the results we help each client achieve;
- *People* - People first in every decision we make;
- *Action* - Because that's what people see, hear, and feel;
- *Community* - Building strong relationships with and between the organizations we serve;
- *Together* - Because no one makes a lasting **IMPACT** by themselves!

I won't begin to pretend that these are perfect, but they're ours. You're welcome to reach out to either of us on any given day if you want to discuss in more detail how we work to model each of these in our lives and through our work.

That said, we wouldn't have been able to have the same kind of conversation around any of our values just a few years ago. We've had to work extremely hard at identifying exactly what we wanted to be known for.

What Will Your IMPACT Look Like?

Early on in this process, as we looked at what happens when foundational values aren't in place (and a few times since), I referenced an article from MIT Sloan Management Review called "When It Comes to Culture, Does Your Company Walk the Talk?[41]", where the authors shared this about how frequently companies share their values:

> "When Johnson & Johnson's CEO codified the company's principles into a credo in 1943, corporate value statements were a novelty. Today they are ubiquitous among large corporations. In our study of nearly 700 large companies, we found that more than 80% published an official set of corporate values on their website. Senior leaders, in particular, love to talk about their company culture. Over the past three decades, more than three-quarters of CEOs interviewed in a major business magazine discussed their company's culture or core values — even when not specifically asked about it. Corporate values statements are nearly universal, but do they matter? Critics dismiss them as cheap talk with no impact on employees' day-to-day behavior."

Along the way, I've also mentioned situations where Cindy and I were providing training for supervisors and managers in their own conference rooms, watching them struggle to list their core organizational values. A few of those times, their values were even painted on the walls around us. Had we only come up with a catchy acronym for how we hoped to **IMPACT** the companies we serve by modeling our own core values and listing them on our website, we could have held our heads high for joining that 80%. Interestingly enough, that's the same percentage that Maxwell says consistently falls short of what's expected of them. Coincidence? I doubt it!

We did take it a step further by defining what each value meant, but so did Enron. The difference lies in how we've worked to answer Henderson's first question—*What do you want to be known for?*—for each of the values we listed by developing a crystal-clear picture of what each means to us in practice:

- *Intentionality* - We are intentional in everything we do, ensuring we make a positive difference daily;

  - o Cindy and I regularly review our workload, the clients we support, and our overall messaging to ensure that everything we do aligns with the clear purpose that drives us. As you can imagine, that often results in pulling away from some things and placing more focus on others.

- *Measurability* - Measuring the results we help each client achieve;

  - o I frequently (like at the end of every lesson we share) tell the story of the HR Manager I worked for, who always tasked me with showing a measurable improvement in productivity or profitability after any event I attended. Profitability matters! If we're not working to help every client we serve achieve increased productivity and profitability through the tools we provide, we don't deserve their trust—or their business.

- *People* - People first in every decision we make;

  - o Cindy and I are both primarily task-oriented (she's a high C-blend, and I'm an extremely high D-blend in terms of the DISC Model of Human Behavior). All too often, organizations are viewed as lifeless entities. That's never the case. The people in those organizations drive results, for good or bad. By placing people first in every decision we make, we've been able to achieve results we would have never seen otherwise. That said, there have been times when not being willing to tolerate people being treated poorly has cost us tremendous amounts of money. I'm willing to sacrifice money; I'm not willing to compromise my character.

- *Action* - Because that's what people see, hear, and feel;

    o One of the first things I learned in behavior-based safety is that attitudes and emotions by themselves cannot be measured. That's why we studied behavior. To simplify this: talk is cheap. We strive to exemplify everything we teach daily, and we accept responsibility when we fall short. We've all heard it said that "Our actions to speak so loudly that no one hears what we're saying." However, when our actions back our words, the people we serve can trust what we say.

- *Community* - Building strong relationships with and between the organizations we serve;

    o Cindy and I have been extraordinarily blessed through the relationships we've been able to develop. We cherish the time we have, whether through the work we do or the friendships we've built, with many of the clients I've mentioned as examples of how they've effectively embodied their core values. Few things give us more fulfillment than having the opportunity to connect good people with good people. Proverbs 27:17 says, "As iron sharpens iron, so one person sharpens another." Be it through our *Executive Leadership Elite Think Tank*, our *IMPACT Leadership Academy,* any public event we host, or just through making personal introductions. We actively work at building a leadership community where everyone involved grows stronger.

- *Together* - Because no one makes a lasting **IMPACT** by themselves!

  o This ties back to *Community*, but I needed a "T" to finish out *IMPACT*... While I'm (kinda) kidding, the reality is that I've never felt like I've been very good at any one thing. That said, I've been blessed beyond measure to have worked with and for many amazing people who have helped me achieve some remarkable things that I never could have accomplished on my own. I tell people all that time that I'd get a hell of a lot of work done if I were in business by myself, but since Cindy is by my side, there's a chance you'll actually like it. The same holds true for what companies can achieve together. Every organization has limited resources, but collaborating with others can give any organization an exponential reach.

I'll stress once more that these are by no means perfect, but we work daily to be known *FOR* each value listed. With these fresh in your mind, how much specificity can you go into about each of your core company values? What do you want to be known for? And how clearly can each of your team members picture (and articulate) this?

This is by no means simple, but it's by far the easiest of Jeff Henderson's three challenging questions. Now, let's look at how important it is to be willing to learn what we're really known for.

What Does Your IMPACT Really Look Like?

As with so many companies where "more than 80% published an official set of corporate values on their website," having definitions posted—or even detailing a picture of what we want those values to mean—makes little impact if that's not what we're actually known for. Wearing a He-Man costume at Halloween didn't turn me into the powerful defender of Eternia, and simply listing the values we want to be known for doesn't necessarily equate to what we're known for.

> **Simply listing the values we want to be known for doesn't necessarily equate to what we're known for.**

In some cases, a disconnect between the two arises from innocently misunderstanding how our teams, or the community we serve, truly perceive how we align with our stated core values. I've seen many scenarios where people in leadership roles are remarkable individuals, and those closest to them avoid having a candid conversation about a mismatch between the stated values and what they're seeing to avoid hurting anyone's feelings.

At times, the disconnect arises also from unmanaged expectations—whether within the organization or with the clients we serve. Sometimes, though, the folks most willing to discuss their company's culture or core values, even when not specifically asked about it, are far more interested in talking a good talk than actually walking a good walk. As we looked at how to rally our teams around our core values, I shared examples of how executives spouting off about how they prioritize others while actively undermining the exact folks they claim to serve can quickly lose the trust of their team members, as well as anyone watching from the outside.

If we're genuinely interested in learning what we're known for— what our impact actually looks like as opposed to just what we want it to look like—we'll need to actively solicit input from folks we can trust to provide us with candid feedback. Make no mistake, though: this isn't as simple as sending out an anonymous survey and calling it done. We'll need to schedule time with people who can and will offer their honest opinions, but we also need to ensure they have the proper perspective on what we're working to achieve, and that they have our best interests at heart. Remember what I shared about "Alliance Feedback," as we discussed removing ambiguity while defining our values?

Cindy and I have hosted large public events and worked with organizations at their locations for over a decade. Early on, I recall seeing individuals who did similar work conclude their sessions by having participants complete a "Satisfaction Survey." These "check yes or no" forms rarely provided any specific feedback on what added value or what could be improved, and there was little to no context for what the participant expected coming into the session. Just as filling in a bubble on an evaluation form is of little help without being tied to actual behavior, someone checking a box to say they liked or disliked a session doesn't provide anything we can build on.

This being the case, I quickly scrapped the widespread surveys and have been very intentional ever since to nail down time with specific participants so I can ask them direct questions. In each case, those participants were individuals with perspectives I could learn from, and I trusted them to be open about their feelings. All too often, folks look for feedback from people they know will back their opinion or stroke their ego. That's not "Alliance Feedback," and it definitely won't help us learn what our impact really looks like.

At this stage in my career, I have at least a dozen people I can reach out to for this candid, specific, and measurable feedback. Whether their input encourages me or it stings, I trust their motives; I know they have my best interests at heart, and I'm entirely sure that they understand the impact I want to be known for. I never take this for granted with regard to our business or any other aspect of my life— not even when my friend told me I was fat!

It's crucial to receive this kind of feedback on what we're really known for, but then we've got to use it in answering Henderson's third question. That takes guts! Before we work through that, though, I'll challenge you to make a list of the folks you can count on to provide you with a clear, honest evaluation of what your impact really looks like, so you have something solid to use as a point of comparison.

Making the Two Match

Developing clarity around our specific, intended impact will require focus. Building strong alliances with trusted sources takes time and incredibly dedicated effort. Having a bunch of folks check a box on a survey won't cut it. Assuming we're willing to do the hard work necessary to achieve each of these, we have a shot at answering Jeff Henderson's third question: *Do they match?*

Previously, as we looked at how living out our values can build a reputation that drives results, I referenced a conversation Cindy and I had with Carly Fiorina in late 2019, where she emphasized the importance of taking a "clear-eyed look at our existing state if we wanted to have any hope of achieving our desired future state." We won't be able to take that clear-eyed look without becoming completely locked in on the answers to each of those first questions: *What do we want to be known for?* and *What are we known for?* Making the comparison, or coming to terms with our current state, is where we'll need to have guts.

While this won't require the same level of courage as racing into a burning building or charging enemy troops, we will need to be brave enough to accept the differences we uncover. The perceptions shared with us may sting, and in some cases, there may be little we can do (or choose to do) to change them. As much as we strive to embody what our values mean to us, there will be times when others have different expectations.

Whether we need to close the gap between what we're doing and what we hope to achieve, or reframe how we manage the expectations a team member or client has around our values, aligning what we want our impact to look like with what that impact really looks like can be a steep hill to climb. But it will never happen without seeking and accepting input, then actively making some changes. Once we've identified the work needed to close any gaps, our job as leaders lies in being absolutely fanatical about instilling our values into every aspect of our organizational culture. Don't sweat it, though; this fanaticism relies far more on consistency than intensity.

Getting Fanatical About Instilling Our Core Values into Our Culture

Let's assume there's a gap between the impact we want to make by living out our core values and the actual impact being made through our team's actions. Even if that gap is incredibly small, there's always room for improvement—assuming we've done the work to solicit the kind of alliance feedback that doesn't just tickle our ears...

As leaders, a significant part of our responsibility is continually providing our teams with a clear understanding of where we are and where we are going. With regards to making sure we truly are known for our values in the way we're striving for, keeping the specific words, the detailed explanations, and the practical example each team member can apply in their own role top-of-mind throughout our organization rests on our shoulders. This requires getting fanatical about instilling our core values into our culture.

> **A significant part of our responsibility
> is continually providing our teams
> with a clear understanding
> of where we are and where we are going.**

Throughout this look at how core values serve as a foundation for any organization, I've frequently referenced what I've seen Craig and Kim do since acquiring the first piece of their family business in September 2021. Quite frankly, I've mentioned it in nearly every lesson or general conversation I've had about core values since then. In one of those conversations a while back, the owners of another company we work closely with seemed overwhelmed. As we talked, one said that they just weren't sure they could ever get to a point where they put as much time into sharing their values with their team as Craig and Kim.

Hearing that made me realize that the examples I'd been using painted a more impressive picture than intended. While the work I had seen Craig and Kim do was indeed uncommon, the results they achieved weren't due to the intensity of their approach but rather to the consistency with which they maintained a detailed understanding of their values before their team. I assured the individuals I was speaking with that they wouldn't need to increase the time they invested with their team members; they'd just need to tweak how that time was being used and be intentional about weaving their values into every conversation.

Like I mentioned as we looked at how great programs are built on strong values, there's no such thing as too much! I recently read *Day*

Trading Attention[42] by Gary Vaynerchuk, which focuses on building a brand and driving sales through social media. He mentioned issuing the same challenge to everyone he spoke with: regardless of their social media posting frequency, they needed to post more. Cindy often has at least five posts scheduled on each of our platforms daily, sometimes even more. If I compare that to a client I worked with several years ago who was adamant that one post a week was more than enough, I'd be proud of myself. That organization is still averaging one post each week on one platform but less than one a month on another, and I hadn't seen any of their posts in my feed for months before writing this. All said, I'd still bet Gary V would challenge me and Cindy the same way he does everyone else.

When it comes to instilling our core values into every aspect of our culture, it's not about how eloquent the font is in our handbooks, or how beautifully and artfully the values are painted on our walls. It won't even matter if we stomp our feet or pound the podium as we rattle off the words in an annual meeting with our entire company. The consistency we use, both in detailing our core values and in modeling the behaviors necessary to make them part of our routine, will always trump an intense spurt with no follow-through. There truly is no such thing as too much communication around our core values. Even then, though, that communication will need to be genuine: we'll need to wear those values on our sleeves.

Wearing Our Values on Our Sleeves (and Everywhere Else)

I remember hearing a story about an old man whose wife was in tears. He reluctantly asked what was wrong, and she replied that he clearly didn't love her anymore because it had been years since he told her so. He scoffed and said, "I told you that I loved you when we got married. I'll let you know if anything changes…"

I can assure you: that won't work in a marriage, or any other relationship we care about. And we definitely won't be able to adopt that old man's approach if we ever want to be known for the values listed in our handbooks or on our walls. There's no such thing as talking about them too often.

But here's a word of caution: empty talk won't make the grade. If we're not willing to put our heart and soul into every message we share about our core values, our team members aren't likely to buy in—and we shouldn't expect them to. Think about it: would you or I rally around some half-baked speech that the person delivering it doesn't believe? To that end, should we even refer to something as a "core value" if we can't confidently and passionately talk about the specifics involved in exemplifying it at the drop of a hat?

> **If we're not willing to put our heart and soul into every message we share about our core values, our team members aren't likely to buy in.**

I realize this will likely put some crusty executives on edge; too many of them have the (mistaken) idea that they need to maintain an image of strength at all costs. This reminds me of a story John Maxwell shared years ago about the work he did with senior managers in a multi-billion-dollar organization. Just before a break, John emphasized the importance of being open about their weaknesses. The head of the team pulled John aside during the break to tell him that, while he had a tremendous amount of respect for him, he disagreed with that statement, and simply couldn't afford to do that with his immediate team, or allow them to do it with their teams.

John chuckled, then explained that his team members were already very aware of his weaknesses. Acknowledging his weaknesses would only set them at ease and allow them to support him in those areas.

The same idea holds true for how we share our message detailing our core values. We absolutely must wear our hearts on our sleeves. To that end, perhaps we should consider wearing our values on our sleeves—and anywhere else we can display them. Before expecting our team members to model those values in all they do, we need to be completely committed to providing the most genuine example we're capable of, in our words, our deeds, and any other way we can share that message.

Since starting our business, I've been fanatical about representing our brand constantly. I rarely go out in public without something that openly displays our logo, the logo of one of our programs, our signature colors, or a combination of all those things. Hell, I even had a pair of Jordan 1s made with our logo on the side. As intentional as I've been, Craig and Kim took it one step further: they had a design created for their company t-shirts that incorporated their core organizational values into an image directly corresponding to the field they're in. Their team members wear those shirts daily, both at work and in their personal lives, and it's one of the few shirts I wear that doesn't feature my logo.

While listing your values on the back of a t-shirt may not fit your business model, I challenge you to identify what you can do to wear your values on your sleeve—and anywhere else you can think of. When our values are truly a part of who we are, this shouldn't be too difficult, and it starts the process of weaving those values into everything we do, internally and externally.

Weaving Our Values into Everything We Do

Assuming you've at least taken to heart the idea that consistency trumps intensity and the importance of wearing our values on our sleeves, we're in a great place. Each is a critical piece in the framework for laying a solid foundation around those core values. And with those in place, we now just need to be intentional about weaving each value into every aspect of what we do.

Before I move on, let me stress once more: taking a few basic steps daily will have a far greater (and longer-lasting) impact than one massive spurt of effort that's not sustained. Quite frankly, that spurt may do more harm than good, especially if our teams see us pounding our chests about something we claim is essential one day, only to not hear us mention it again in the following weeks or months.

Early in my manufacturing career, I heard the term "flavor of the month" used as a label for the latest and greatest corporate initiative that was going to revolutionize everything we did. It wasn't long until I understood why so many things received that title: most started with a flurry of activity and excitement, or at least emphasis, but few were ever maintained long enough to produce measurable results. No single group of folks held complete responsibility for any particular initiative falling flat unless we consider Maxwell's statement that "Everything rises and falls on leadership."

Looking back, though, the one common theme I can point to would be that most of those were being pushed from a land far, far away (the corporate HQ) by people who rarely (if ever) set foot in our facility, with the expectation of massive immediate changes, but no plan for ongoing sustainability. The one process that stuck around was the behavior-based safety process I was involved in. I'm certainly not taking credit for that, at least not initially, since I didn't take the reigns until it had been in place for close to three years; few other initiatives ever made it that long. I believe its sticking power rested on getting a lot of people involved while asking for very little support from each.

Weaving our core values into every aspect of how our organizations do business will rest solely on our shoulders, to begin with. However, when we can effectively communicate how each value ties to the work we do and the work our team members do daily, our load becomes significantly lighter. Our consistent message and example will, sooner or later, spill over into what each individual on our team does. While this may seem like a slow and painful process at first, the impact will eventually be exponential - inside our organization and with everyone we deal with externally.

> **When we can effectively communicate how each value ties to the work we do and the work our team members do daily, our load becomes significantly lighter.**

Just in case I haven't stressed it enough, sharing a simple, consistent message around our core values carries far more weight than a parade of pomp and circumstance that we never refer to again. My challenge to you here is to get incredibly intentional about how you weave your company's core values into everything you say and do, then make sure you have a system (or maybe even a dedicated person) for holding you accountable to sticking with your messaging and example until it becomes a part of who you are. This will serve as the framework for laying your foundation. Then, you'll just need to add some bracing to make sure everything stays in place.

Everything, According to Our Values

Having detailed why a framework for building the foundation of our organizations around our core values is so important, as well as the three simple steps to serve as the framework— consistent communication, keeping our values visible all the time, and intentionally weaving them into every aspect of our operation— there's one thing left to work through. It's the most critical piece of making anything we've done stick. We absolutely must develop the discipline to do everything, every single day, according to our core values.

> **We absolutely must develop the discipline to do everything, every single day, according to our core values.**

As we began this examination of the role values play, I shared my experience from early 2022, which has served as a textbook example of how quickly leaders changed the culture in a 75-year-old organization by applying those three steps. The consistent, heartfelt approach Craig and Kim used earned buy-in from even the most tenured team members, where a forced intensity would have likely had the effect of swatting a fly on someone's forehead—with a hammer! I mentioned it earlier, but it's worth sharing again for emphasis: the Bureau of Labor Statistics reports the annual average for voluntary turnover is just shy of twenty-five percent across all industries. Using their core values as the foundation for everything they did, from the day they acquired the company, resulted in just five percent voluntary turnover over *two years*.

In his book *Traction*[43], Gino Wickman says, "Once they're defined, you must hire, fire, review, reward, and recognize people based on these core values. This is how to build a thriving culture around them." To date, I've been involved in nearly every hiring decision Craig and Kim have made—not because I necessarily enjoy that work at this point or have time in my schedule, but because I know the atmosphere they will provide for anyone joining their team. We've been fortunate to interact with a steady stream of qualified candidates for nearly every position that has been open, as well as for some positions that weren't open. Regardless of qualifications, though, we've been cautious to look for a match in values. Quite frankly, that's something Cindy and I have observed in many of the organizations I've cited as examples throughout this process. However, even when this is top of mind throughout the onboarding process, no one gets it right every time.

> **Once they're defined, you must hire, fire, review, reward, and recognize people based on these core values.**

Wickman's suggestion to "review, reward, and recognize people based on these core values" should be almost automatic if we've developed the discipline to truly weave our values into all that we do.

The firing part, though, has been the part even the toughest and crustiest executives struggle with. Truth be told, I initially struggled with that, too. Although terminations are often considered "involuntary turnover" in studies like the one from the BLS, I would submit to you that, when someone repeatedly chooses behavior that isn't aligned with the core values, we detailed and modeled, any disciplinary action or termination that follows is absolutely voluntary. When our foundation is truly built on our values, everything else becomes simple; our decisions are made by observing the behaviors each team member (candidate or client) exhibits.

Notice I said everything else is *simple*; not *easy*! The best leaders I've had the privilege of being around have genuinely cared for every member of their teams. Even when someone repeatedly chooses to violate our core values, it can be incredibly hard (at least mentally and emotionally) to hold them accountable. However, when we consistently make every other decision based on those core values, momentum *will* build.

Consistency Builds Momentum

Let's consider Gino Wickman's statement again: "Once they're defined, you must hire, fire, review, reward, and recognize people based on these core values. This is how to build a thriving culture around them." If we're willing to take this to heart and consistently act in accordance with our values, momentum will build.

I'd love to claim that this will be easy and happen immediately, but that's just not how things work. In every industry, there's always that one example that seems to wreck the curve, appearing to be the overnight model of perfection. We've all heard the phrase, "The grass is always greener on the other side of the fence." While that may indeed be what we see from a distance, my three and a half decades in the workplace, and over twenty-five years studying leadership, have shown me that the grass in those organizations becomes that green in one of two ways: it's growing over top a septic field, or someone put in a hell of a lot of work to make it that way.

If you've always lived in a metropolitan area and are unfamiliar with a septic field, I'll paint you a picture. Cindy and I live in a rural area that lacks municipal water and sewer systems. Our water comes from a well, and a septic system was installed as our home was built. In the driest weeks of summer, our grass becomes very crispy and brown, except directly above the seven drain lines from our septic tank. (Thank God our well has provided a steady flow of water through it all.) All the used water, along with everything else that goes down the drain or gets flushed, is processed through the septic tank located just outside the house, and the liquid is dispersed through those lines. I'll spare you the complete lesson on how it all works, but, as you can imagine, we wouldn't want to plant a garden in that area regardless of how green the grass remains. To keep the rest of our two-and-a-half acres green all summer long would be a monumental undertaking.

The companies that have built thriving cultures around their core values by developing the discipline to "hire, fire, review, reward, and recognize people based on these core values" are those where the leaders, often just one or two to begin with, have invested a tremendous amount effort to build the momentum necessary to get anyone else's buy-in. However, as those leaders have consistently done so over time, and the leaders they've worked to develop around them follow suit, that momentum builds—often much slower than anyone would like. In the cases where that green grass is over top of the septic field, where a magical culture appears to have popped up overnight, the fresh vegetables served at the company picnic will eventually taste like the crap they were grown in...

If you've ever noticed how perfect a Major League Baseball field looks, just know it's not by accident. Not only are entire teams of people involved in getting it to that point and maintaining it, but they're also very protective of their work. Only the players go on the field, and only just before and during the games. They don't practice there in the off-season. And those fields are covered during any other events hosted in the ballpark. If I put all that time, effort, and money into making my yard look that nice, I sure wouldn't want my neighbors' kids or dogs doing their business on it. When we've done the work to build our values into our culture, and we've finally built momentum around those values, we'll need to be just as protective as the groundskeepers at a Major League ballpark, or Clint Eastwood with his lawn.

Protect Our Culture (and Values) at All Cost

If you've been disciplined enough to consistently (and fanatically) follow the simple framework for instilling core values organization's culture, I have no doubt that your grass is at least starting to show its greener hues. And the steps you've taken will serve to eliminate even the slightest perception of that green grass being over top of a septic field, at least for anyone being remotely honest with themselves.

That said, a reality every leader will eventually face is the need to deal with individuals who simply don't share the same values. I've shared examples several times detailing how some of the best leaders and business owners I've had the privilege of supporting have passed up extremely talented candidates because they didn't feel like those candidates matched their organizational values. The challenge is that even the most comprehensive interview process will only reveal so much.

> **A reality every leader will eventually face
> is the need to deal with individuals
> who simply don't share the same values.**

Jack Welch, the former CEO of General Electric, who was known for his keen ability to identify and hire great candidates, once said that even the best only make the right hires fifty percent of the time. I'm certainly not going to argue his numbers. While I've never considered myself the best at interviewing or identifying great potential team members, I do believe I've become quite skilled at it through practice. Like any skill we develop through repetition, recognizing a match with our values is a skill that can be honed. Even then, though, there will be times when we miss a glaring flag, or we just get it wrong. There will also be times when something changes in a team member's life, and they no longer align with our core values—even if they did for years prior.

Regardless of when we recognize the mismatch, how it comes to our attention, or when it occurs in the relationship, part of our responsibility as leaders is to address it directly and swiftly. Earlier, as I emphasized that expectations without accountability are empty talk, I made a point that I'll revisit once more because it's so often misunderstood: addressing an issue that isn't aligned with our core values doesn't always involve formal disciplinary action. In many cases, a team member who misses the mark has, at least in their mind, a very legitimate reason for their action. However, we must absolutely discuss it, explain the mismatch, and outline what we need from them moving forward. We'll also need to be clear about the path they'll be choosing if they don't make the expected changes.

Everything I've worked with Craig and Kim on since mid-2021 has been aligned with the core values they held when they purchased their first business, and they've now built all their businesses around them. Even with the exceptionally low voluntary turnover they've experienced (I can only think of a handful of folks who have left their organizations for other jobs), there have been a few situations where we've had to part ways with team members. None of those, though, were decisions we made. In fact, every single one was based on decisions that team members made continually, which did not align with or represent those clearly defined and consistently exemplified core values. In each case, the decisions were tough on a personal level. However, to protect the culture they were working so hard to build, there was no room for compromise on those values.

Although I've mentioned Craig and Kim repeatedly throughout this process, I'm not about to suggest they're perfect, or that their organization is the only one I've seen with a strong foundation built on core values. What I will say, though, is that they've been entirely transparent in every issue we've discussed. They immediately accept responsibility for any problem that arising across their whole organizations—and all of that has been based on the core values they discussed with me in our first conversation.

As impressed as I've been with the example Craig and Kim have set, they're not superstars. They've just been incredibly consistent (some may even say *fanatical*) in modeling their core values. They've built those values into every possible aspect of what each of their team members do, and they've worked diligently to protect the culture they've built around those values at all costs. You could say they've followed a simple framework for building their business on values. The beauty is that it's something any other leader can apply in their organizations! Hopefully, the steps we've worked through here provide you with everything you need to lay a strong foundation for your own business built on values.

APPENDIX

REAL-WORLD EXAMPLES

The "Real-World Examples" appendix brings the principles of *The Values Advantage* to life through stories from leaders the author has worked with directly. In this final section, you'll learn how these leaders have built their core values into three specific aspects of their organizations. These case studies detail specific actions and measurable results, from increased profitability to stronger team cultures, and how they've woven core values into serving clients and communities, showcasing broader impact. These real-world examples, drawn from diverse industries, illustrate the framework from Chapter 11 in action, inspiring readers to apply values-driven leadership in their own organizations and reinforcing the book's call to build a lasting legacy.

Identifying Your Core Values

The Power of Core Values to Change an Organization

In September 2016, after over 28 years of military service, I had the privilege and honor of serving my fellow Veterans by leading Virginia's Jobs for Veteran Grant program (JVSG). This program's singular goal is to provide funding to States so that they can hire specialized staff who deliver intensive one on one career and training-related services to eligible veterans and spouses. The idea is a simple one, beginning with President Abraham Lincoln, we as a nation promised "To care for him who shall have borne the battle, and for his widow, and his orphan. Those of us who are part of the JVSG program help keep that promise by securing employment for Veterans and eligible spouses, including special disabled Veterans, disabled Veterans, economically or educationally disadvantaged Veterans, and Veterans with other barriers to employment.

When I assumed responsibility for the program in September 2016, it was transitioning in an effort to better serve the Veterans of the Commonwealth. And like any organization that is in a state of transition, we first needed to define who we were as a program and what type of culture we wanted to create. My initial step was to identify and hire three (3) regional leaders who would help lead this organization so that we as an organization could reach our full potential and in turn maximize our service to Virginia's Veterans. This process required deep self-reflection, beginning with clarifying my own personal values—values shaped by my faith in God and my service as an officer in the U.S. Army.

I identified five personal key values: marriage, spiritual life, family and children, work and Church/Ministry. These key values are undergirded by three **core values: Covenant relationships, Integrity, and loving/fearing God** with all of my being. With these guiding principles, I sought and found leaders whose values aligned with mine, understanding that such alignment is essential for fostering a cohesive and productive organizational culture.

I think it is important that we are always mindful of the intricate dance of leadership and management, with respect to the alignment between personal and organizational values. Research affirms that this alignment is a pivotal factor not only for the harmony of the workplace but also for its success and sustainability. Core values, whether they belong to individuals or entire organizations, serve as the guiding stars that inform decisions, shape behaviors, and set the foundational ethos of an organization's environment. It is this this alignment, or at times the lack thereof, that plays a critical role in defining the trajectory of both leaders and the organization he/she leads.

Initially, my team and I embraced eight core values: **Respect, Integrity, Commitment, Collaboration, Client Focused, Selfless Service, Excellence, and One Team One Fight**.

During the first two years of this transition, we had what I believe to be God guided encounters and opportunities to receive training and in some ways mentorship from the Doves as well as exposure to the teachings of John Maxwell.

One of the great lessons learned was to allow the organization and its team members to help shape and hone the Core values. We listened and revamped those Core values in 2018 to five: **Selfless Service, Veteran Centric, Intentional, Resilient and Servant Leadership.**

I believe embracing and embodying these Core values has propelled Virginia's JVSG program from being ranked in the high forties to consistently one of the top ten programs in the country. It is our core values that distinguish us in the eyes of Veterans, stakeholders, team members, and federal program leaders. More than policies or procedures, it is the power of values—lived out daily—that transforms organizations!

LTC (Ret) Dr. Robert M Walker, Jr., Dmin, MDIV, MA MFT
Director of Workforce Services Operations
Virginia Employment Commission

Engineering for a Better World

When I started Colman Engineering back in early 2010, I knew what was important to me. I wanted to do things right, without cutting corners. I wanted to treat everyone—especially regulators, whose role is to push back—with kindness and respect. And I wanted to be honest, especially when it comes to price quotes and setting timeframe expectations.

These values were important to me because they are how I naturally operate. And I had seen that other firms weren't operating this way. I wanted to draw a line in the sand and say, "This is how Colman Engineering will operate." At this point, I didn't realize I was "identifying our core values"—but that's essentially what I was doing.

For the first few years, it was relatively easy to operate according to these values because I was the only employee. As I started growing the team, I had to instill these values by demonstrating how I wanted us to operate and by pointing out actions that didn't align. But we still hadn't put our values into words or identified them as actual values.

Fast-forward to 2021, and Wes and Cindy invited us to participate in a values workshop they were conducting. In that workshop, everyone worked together to nail down exactly what is important to us as an organization and put it all into words. When I saw the final product, I saw that the values were—surprisingly, not surprisingly—consistent with the values I had established from the start.

We posted the values and would talk about them when needed—especially when we saw actions that needed correction. But in 2024, with encouragement from Wes and Cindy, we took our values initiative to the next level.

We assigned one person to be the "champion" of our values. That person now has a 5-minute segment ("Values Corner") during our weekly all-team meeting, where she engages the team in a conversation about our values. Although 5 minutes doesn't sound like a lot, we've found that it's enough to keep our values front and center and keep the conversation going.

We've also updated our values poster, which now includes actionable steps we can all take to live out each value. We've posted them all over the office, so you can't go far without seeing one!

We've also integrated our values into our annual performance review process. This helps provide additional accountability while also demonstrating that we care as much (or more) about our values as we do about actual work performance.

As a result, we're building a company culture where values aren't just words on a wall—they're part of our everyday vocabulary, shaping how we work, how we treat each other, and how our clients and partners experience Colman Engineering every day.

Gil Colman, PE
President & CEO,
Colman Engineering

Identifying Core Values: A Transformative Journey at New Creation VA

At New Creation VA, a nonprofit dedicated to counteracting human trafficking, we recognized that our mission to prevent exploitation, provide dignified opportunities, and mobilize communities hinged on more than just our programs—it required a team deeply aligned with our values. Many times in the nonprofit world, our missions are clear, but our values are not! That gap can become a barrier to our work and the way we engage our communities! As we prepare to launch a new social enterprise—a coffee shop and café to build workforce skills for underserved women—the need to lead with consistency has become undeniable.

The process of identifying our core values began with intentional listening within our Leadership Team. We posed critical questions: *What values define our work? What traits make a great team member? How should survivors, partners, and the community experience us?* Initially, we compiled a broad list—faith, kindness, generosity, and innovation—but themes soon emerged. Through collaborative exercises, Authenticity rose to the top. We committed to showing up honestly in every interaction, whether with those we serve, donors, customers, or the community.

We used anonymous input, sticky-note exercises, story-sharing from our ministry experiences, and group reflection to refine our list. A pivotal moment came when we debated "righteousness." Some feared it might be misread as self-righteousness or judgment, clashing with the grace and mercy we aimed to embody. This insight shifted our focus to values reflecting our true intent. After multiple meetings and conversations we landed on our six guiding values— Integrity, Authenticity, Justice, Empowerment, Awareness, and Servanthood—serving as a shared language for decision-making.

Naming and defining our values has brought clarity and alignment across our organization. Team members feel equipped to lead with consistency, even in challenging moments. Perhaps the most powerful outcome came from a survivor who shared, "I finally found the place I belong." It made me realize that we are successfully creating an environment where women feel safe, seen, and empowered.

The key takeaway is that identifying core values isn't a one-time task—it's an ongoing commitment to self-awareness and alignment. This process clarified our purpose, enabling us to lead with intention and inspire our community.

As we look ahead, I'm reminded of a defining moment that occurred during a workshop with an organization we're modeling our café after, prompting us to explore how values could shape its future structure and programming: asking *how these values will guide our café's programming?* It's a question that echoes the original challenge—how will our values shape not just our work but the lives we touch?

For any organization, taking time to listen, reflect, and define what matters can unlock transformative potential, much like the grace and mercy we strive to embody. This effort, though demanding, promises fulfillment and impact that far outweigh easier paths, as we lead with purpose every step of the way.

For perspective, here's how we've defined our core values:

Integrity: We act with honesty, transparency, + accountability in all we do. We honor our commitments, steward resources responsibly, + ensure our actions align with our mission + values — even when no one is watching.

Authenticity: We show up with honesty + vulnerability, creating space for people to bring their whole selves. We value genuine relationships, celebrate uniqueness + reject pretense or performance.

Justice: We work to dismantle systems of exploitation, striving for fairness + dignity. We advocate for lasting change that restores what is broken + confronts what is harmful.

Empowerment: We believe every person holds inherent worth + potential. We walk alongside survivors + communities, equipping them with tools, resources, + opportunities to thrive + lead.

Awareness: We commit to listening, learning, + educating others. We shine light on hidden injustices, elevate survivor voices, + inspire collective action through knowledge + understanding.

Servanthood: We lead by serving others first. With humility + compassion, we seek to uplift, support, + sacrifice for the good of those around us, putting people before position, power + profit.

Sabrina Dorman-Andrew
Co-Founder + Executive Director
New Creation VA

Embodying Your Core Values

CASCADE in Action: How Lived Values Saved Deals, Earned Trust, and Became a True Competitive Edge

As the CEO of a multi-million-dollar company, you have countless opportunities to demonstrate your leadership and beliefs every day. One of the most consequential—both for the present and future of the company—is defining the values that I, along with my management team, believe are the essence of our mission.

These values must be part of everyday life—intentional and actionable. They should be created by the team that will lead the company, avoiding fancy corporate jargon that sounds "cool" but means nothing to the rest of the organization. These values should speak for themselves to employees, stakeholders, and customers.

At BR Printers, our **CASCADE** values aren't a poster in the break room. It's what we actually do when the pressure is on. Our national footprint serves diverse industries, from education to luxury brands, providing efficient, scalable production. These values, which were instituted when our team came together in early 2024, aren't just words on a slide; they're lived daily through our actions. Below are specific real-world examples from our operations that illustrate how we enact and live each one, providing inspiration for our team to continue excelling and a guiding light on all we do!.

Customer-Centric means we stop thinking like a vendor and start thinking like the client's teammate. Last spring an educational publisher came to us with a large problem —new interactive workbooks with AR features, crazy deadline, and specs that didn't quite add up. Instead of just quoting the job, we jumped on calls, sketched QR layouts together, and shipped prototypes two weeks early. Teachers loved them, sales jumped 20%, and the client said we basically saved their year.

Agile is what kept a luxury brand's holiday launch alive in 2023 during the supply chain disruptions created by strikes in the West Coast ports. Rigid-box stock was nowhere to be found. Our sourcing crew found a better, greener domestic board in hours, rerouted press schedules across two plants, and never missed a beat. The boxes hit counters on time and looked incredible.

Solutions Innovators shows up when we refuse to just "fill the order." A Publisher asked us to kit classroom samples, but their old data showed weak response rates. We dug into the numbers, redesigned the inserts by region, and handed them a 35% lift in engagement. Same budget, way better results.

Collaboration means two teams who've never met in person crushing a web-to-print portal for a big nonprofit. Designers, coders, fulfillment folks—weekly huddles and one junior designer's drag-and-drop idea made it to production because everyone actually listened. Launch day was flawless; client orders now turn in half the time.

Alignment is East Coast and West Coast plants moving like one machine. A massive state textbook rollout had us syncing schedules across four time zones and 2 printing plants, standardizing quality checks, and trimming freight costs by pooling trucks. Zero defects, delivered early, and the program director sent us a thank-you note we still have pinned up in San Jose.

Data-driven problem-solvers is using real numbers instead of hunches. A children's publisher kept missing delivery windows. We pulled all available run data, spotted bottlenecks in binding and trimming, tweaked the sequence, and shaved 25% off lead times without touching quality. They're still using the new schedule we built.

Experienced Integrity is the moment everyone remembers on a big children's book run. The client pushed hard to cut costs on ink and binding to hit a price point. Our operations vets knew the cheaper stuff wouldn't meet safety specs. They shut the job down, walked the client through the risk, and held the line. Client changed its specs, books flew off shelves, no recalls, no nightmares. Trust earned.

That's **CASCADE** in the wild—not theory, not buzzwords. It's late nights, fast decisions, and choosing the right thing even when it's the harder thing. It's why clients stick with us and why we're proud to wear the BR logo every day.

Jorge Velasco
President, CEO
BR Printers

Living Values Through Recognition: Augusta Health's Values Award

At Augusta Health, we often say our values are more than words on a wall — they are the compass guiding how we care for patients, support our community, and uplift one another. In the fast-paced world of healthcare, where every day brings new challenges, values can feel abstract unless we make them tangible. One of the most powerful ways we bring them to life is through our quarterly Values Award, a recognition program that celebrates teammates who embody our core values: Patient and Community Centeredness, Excellence, Professionalism, and Teamwork.

The "Augusta Health Way" defines how we live these values. It shapes our culture, inspires trust, and provides the foundation for excellence. It's not only about what we do, but how we do it — caring with compassion, leading with integrity, and working together with purpose.

Unlike many awards given from the top down, the Values Award is driven by the voices of our people. Anyone — patients, board members, volunteers, nurses, physicians, or team members — can nominate a colleague or team. The process is intentionally simple: identify who, choose the value they lived out, and tell the story. These stories are the heartbeat of the award, turning everyday actions into lasting lessons of what it means to serve with values.

One powerful story came from the Emergency Department. An ED nurse, cared for a woman after a motor vehicle accident on what was supposed to be a milestone day — the patient and her husband were scheduled for a critical fertility appointment. The nurse not only treated her medical needs but also offered empathy, reassurance, and a shared human connection during a vulnerable moment. Months later, the couple welcomed a healthy baby girl — and named her Savannah, in honor of the nurse who had stood by them in their time of need. This extraordinary gesture reflects the profound and lasting impact of compassionate care, reminding us that even brief encounters can shape lives forever.

Another example highlights teamwork at its finest. When severe flooding struck Augusta Health's childcare building, the Facilities Team immediately mobilized — moving furniture, coordinating repairs, and restoring safety. At the very same time, other maintenance team members worked through the night to repair a failed cooling system, sourcing parts, delivering fans, and ensuring patient and staff comfort. These back-to-back crises could have easily overwhelmed any team, yet their resilience, communication, and collaboration turned obstacles into opportunities to live out our values. Their work not only safeguarded operations but also modeled the power of teamwork — proving that even behind-the-scenes roles are essential to our mission.

These quarterly celebrations have become cultural touchstones. Leaders attend alongside staff and families, creating moments of pride and connection that ripple across the organization. To further amplify their impact, each Values Award winner has their professional photograph and story displayed in the cafeteria — a daily reminder for every team member, visitor, and leader that values are lived here. These visible examples encourage others to pause, reflect, and consider how they too can carry forward the Augusta Health Way.

For leaders, the Values Award is more than recognition. It is a deliberate investment in culture, a way to signal that values are not aspirational but essential. By lifting up real stories, leaders make values tangible and inspire others to follow. Over time, this recognition builds a shared language of behaviors, creating clarity around what "Excellence" or "Professionalism" truly look like in action.

The impact is profound. Employees begin to seek out values in one another, not just to nominate but to emulate. Engagement grows, retention strengthens, and the organization becomes more deeply aligned with its mission. In a time when healthcare faces workforce burnout and high turnover, the Values Award is not simply a "feel-good" initiative — it is a leadership tool that anchors our culture and ensures every patient encounter reflects the values we hold dear.

At Augusta Health, we have learned this truth: when you shine a light on values lived out loud, they multiply. Recognition becomes more than applause — it becomes a strategy for leading with values every day.

Crystal Farmer
Sr. VP, COO
Augusta Health

Leading with P.R.I.D.E.: A Police Chief's Commitment to Community-First Values

I've spent 16 years in law enforcement and have seen every shade of policing—good, bad, and in between. The difference isn't just in the actions; it's in the heart and values behind them. Excellent policing starts with one simple truth: put others before yourself. We exist to serve the community, not ourselves. A police department is like a family, but if we ever place our needs above the citizens we protect, we wouldn't run toward danger for them. As chief, I make every decision with community first, department second. That's sometimes different from a for-profit business; our business is to protect and serve.

On SWAT, we followed a priority-of-life scale: citizen #1, officer #2, suspect #3. That scale drove every choice. Everything we do at Bridgewater Police Department flows from our values, captured in the acronym P.R.I.D.E.—a daily reminder to take pride in our service to the community, our department, and the profession.

P – Professionalism. We bring it to every task, high-stakes or routine. Professionalism isn't selective; it extends to the suspect just as much as the victim or witness. Honesty is non-negotiable. We won't lie to a citizen—we'll tell the truth and guide them forward.

R – Respect. Respect isn't earned; it's required. I once watched a suspect who'd abducted a four-year-old and shot at officers during a chase at triple-digit speeds. In custody, he mocked us with foul language and laughed at the chaos he'd caused. The easy path was to mirror his contempt.

Instead, we called him "sir" and walked him through the arrest process with dignity. Respect held firm, even when it wasn't returned.

**I – Integrity.*• It's doing the right thing when no one's watching. Power tempts; I've been offered favors and so have countless officers. History has shown it ends badly—on the news, in the mirror, or both. Integrity isn't optional; it's the only way to live with yourself.

**D – Dedication.*• This isn't taught; it's inside you. It's choosing the community's needs over your own agenda. In 2022, an active shooter struck Bridgewater College. I was tied up with the suspect and hadn't called for backup. Before I knew it, every off-duty officer was there— volunteering, helping, going far beyond the call. That's dedication in action.

**E – Excellence.*• Complacency kills progress. Excellence demands discipline: constant training, accountability, physical fitness, learning from mistakes, and staying humble. No one accidentally becomes a great officer, and no department stumbles into being a model agency. I've heard before, you don't save money by accident; you plan and execute. Same with excellence—you pursue it intentionally, every shift.

Our vision statement includes a question we ask ourselves daily: "What more can I do?" It's not about what we can get; it's about what we can give. That mindset—community first—anchors everything. We swore an oath, and P.R.I.D.E. is how we keep it.

Chief Phillip Read
Chief of Police,
Bridgewater Police Department

Embodying Insperity's Core Values as a Leader for Our Team and Our Clients

As District Manager of Insperity's DC1 office, I don't just talk about our core values—I strive to embody **Integrity, Caring, Innovation, Teamwork, and Excellence** every single day so my team sees exactly what leadership looks like when values drive action. When I live them, they have an example to follow. When they follow, our clients experience the difference.

Integrity is the bedrock, and it has to start with me. Every client interaction, every internal decision, every tough conversation must pass the transparency test. A prospective client recently wavered about leaving their longtime provider. Instead of pushing a polished pitch, I gathered my leadership team and built a brutally honest side-by-side comparison: every strength, every weakness, every risk clearly laid out. No fluff. No omission. They signed with Insperity not because we out-sold the competition, but because we out-truthed them. I drill this into my team weekly: *Do the right thing. If you don't know what "right" is, ask.*

Caring isn't a buzzword; it's a leadership requirement. When a colleague faced a personal hardship, I didn't delegate empathy—I led it. As a team, we rallied around them; covering meetings, checking in with them personally, and ensuring they felt valued. That same heart shapes how we serve clients. One small business owner confided in me about burnout. Instead of pushing a product, I paused to listen, then connected them with resources to help ease their load. *Caring isn't optional. It's how trust is built, one human moment at a time.*

Innovation drives me to continually improve, and I emphasis this with my team. We don't settle for "how it's always been done." Recently, our team piloted a new onboarding process for clients that streamlined paperwork and improved clarity. The feedback was overwhelmingly positive, and it's now being considered for broader implementation. Innovation isn't just about technology—it's about finding smarter, more human-centered ways to serve. *If it doesn't make the client's life easier or our work sharper, it doesn't belong here.*

Teamwork is our engine, and I fuel that with the "we before me" mindset. Whether it's sharing insights from a client meeting or jumping in to help with a proposal, collaboration is second nature. I've seen firsthand how cross-functional teamwork—between advisors, HR specialists, and client service managers—creates a seamless experience for our clients. It's not about who gets credit; it's about delivering results together. My constant reminder: *Get the client where they need to go, and we all get where we need to be.*

Excellence is the standard I inspect daily. our standard. We don't aim to meet expectations—we aim to exceed them. That means being prepared, responsive, and proactive. One client recently shared that our team's attention to detail helped them avoid a costly compliance issue. That kind of feedback reinforces why we hold ourselves to such high standards. *Excellence isn't perfection—it's consistent execution of the right thing, the right way, every time.*

By embodying these values, we don't just serve our clients—we strengthen our relationships, build trust, and create impact. These values aren't slogans on a wall; they're the behaviors we choose every day. And when we live them fully, we become not just advisors, but partners in our clients' success.

To distill it down, it's about sincerity, reliability and competency. Do what you say you're going to do when you say you're going to do it, not just some of the time but all of the time!

Larry Cain
District Manager,
Insperity

Building Our Core Values Into How We Serve Our Clients & Community

Connecting Through Core Values: Building Community Trust and Safety

Within the Frederick County Fire & Rescue Department I carry dual roles as a Deputy Fire Chief and the Emergency Management Coordinator. As a Deputy Fire Chief, I lead strategic planning for a rapidly growing fire & rescue department with nearly 200 personnel across 13 work locations, including 11 operational firehouses and an additional firehouse currently in the architectural design phase. As the Emergency Management Coordinator, I lead disaster and emergency preparedness planning to ensure the health, safety, and well-being of approximately 100,000 residents across Frederick County's 416 square miles. These are important roles, but they are not my only roles of importance!

Outside of emergency services, I am a husband and father and serve as a Boy Scout leader for my twin sons, spending time together adventuring outdoors. As a Boy Scout leader, I recently served on the training staff for Wood Badge, the premier leadership development program for adult leaders in Scouting. A key exercise in the program is known as the Values Game. Participants are provided with 38 cards, each listing a different core value. They are given time to review each of the cards and then are asked to select the 10 values most important to them. The cards are further sorted into the top 5 and then the top 3 values most important to each individual participant. This essential exercise helps participants determine the values central to their beliefs, their core values.

As I guided a small but diverse group through the exercise, trends emerged as core values began to align among the participants. Family, fun, and volunteerism/service all appeared in the top 10 values for each participant. No surprise, considering the participants are all dedicated volunteer leaders supporting their children in scouting. Their values coalesced around their core purpose.

Could the same exercise attain similar results in emergency services? Without question it would! Firefighters, EMT's, paramedics, dispatchers, and law enforcement officers all share a core purpose. We protect our neighbors from danger and save the lives of those in peril. There are core values associated with that purpose, such as courage, commitment, teamwork, integrity, and trust. Indeed, those core values are represented in Frederick County Fire & Rescue's organizational core values.

The members of our organization and the Frederick County community care deeply about the core values we hold as a fire & rescue department. The core values guide not only our actions in times of emergency, but how we work together, how we make ourselves better, and how we support our community before, during, and after emergencies. The core values define who we are and what we do.

Our core values provide a strong foundation in who we are, but it is our culture that carries us forward each day in what we do. Culture puts into action our shared core values. Culture is how we hold ourselves accountable to live up to our values. It's how we show up early each shift, readying our protective equipment for the next emergency, disciplining our bodies through physical fitness and our minds through education. It's also how we take time, even in so serious a profession, to cook meals as a crew, to bring our families together in friendship, and it's how we always find joy in welcoming children as visitors in our home away from home.

In a business sense, values are crucial to the success of an organization. Even more crucial is the importance of values to people, both the ones we work with and the ones we serve. Our values, and our culture, connect the people in the big red truck to the businesses and houses in our community and the people inside them. As a leader, you must ensure that your values and culture connect your organization with your community. It carries success beyond just dollars and cents and into the hearts of people.

Ben G. Coffman MA, EFO NRP
Deputy Fire Chief – Emergency Management Coordinator
Frederick County, Virginia

Integrity, Community, Excellence: How Pioneer Bank Made Its Values Matter Again

Pioneer Bank is a local community bank that was founded in Stanley, VA in 1909. The bank has offices located in Stanley, Luray, Shenandoah, Ruckersville, Charlottesville, and Harrisonburg. I am a Senior Vice President and serve in the role of Market President for Harrisonburg and Rockingham County. Pioneer takes pride in the markets we serve and holds our customers and employees in high esteem. Our core values provide us with the foundation to deliver products and services in the communities we serve.

Integrity – A first for us is to carry out each and every day with honesty and strong moral principles. We want our customers to know that all transactions are backed with this core value. This is a standard that we must have and treat as non-negotiable. In the financial industry, trusted relationships are built around this. I want our communities to know we care and will provide trusted financial solutions for them.

Community – This value is one that makes us who we are. We live, work, and play in the communities we serve, and it is important that we support them. We spend countless hours volunteering in many ways. This can be serving on civic boards or coaching youth sports. We also believe that monetary support to our communities is important and helpful as we want to watch them succeed. Customers want to know that we are invested in their locality, not just providing services.

Excellence – The above and beyond of what we do daily. We not only work to be precise, accurate, and responsive, but we want to live this out above and beyond in our customer service. This value is a standout and something we really want to be recognized for. Financials institutions are somewhat similar in products and services, so providing excellence in our delivery is what we work hard to achieve.

Here at Pioneer, we have taken initiative in the second half of 2025 to evaluate these values and consider if we really were living them out. Through much discussion, it was evident that we were not implementing them into our communications, meetings, or daily tasks. It was clear that they were just writing on the wall and not embodying how we wanted our brand to be lived.

We have worked hard to re-engage our employees with our core values and to enhance them with any new hires. We are now spotlighting employees from recognition they receive around our core values from their colleagues and customers. This is happening with bank wide email recognition. In addition, we have started a "Coin" campaign. This campaign is designed around the bronze, silver, and gold coin status. These coins are very limited and rewarded in above and beyond value recognitions. Bronze is rewarded at the management level, silver is rewarded from our senior management, and the gold can only be given by our CEO. These coins will be rewarded with monetary bonuses at the end of each quarter as a thank you for their commitment and dedication to Pioneer Bank. This has really sparked the morale and comradery of our employees. I believe this implementation has given us an awareness of how we interact and carry out our daily duties with both internal and external customers.

In addition to the spotlight, we hold an annual service day in January on a bank holiday so all employees can be together at the same time. In 2026, we specifically awarded employees who were nominated the most by their colleagues and represented each of our three core values with an award issued for each.

I have learned that you can write out or post what you think your organization should be or look like, but are they really being carried out? I would honestly say that we were not, and I am sure many businesses are not. Taking the time to evaluate your core values to see how they are lived out is worth the mission. If they are not or if they are, just not who you thought they were, change them. The key is not only to value your business, but to truly live those out from the top down. There is never enough communication around your values. Success is driven by your employees who simply excel in them, consistently modeling those values to the communities we serve.

Josh Hale
SVP/Market President
Pioneer Bank

Empowering Through Values: How The Power Connection Turns Employees into Partners

As the Chief Enabler at the Power Connection, I view my primary responsibility is to lead the team to be empowered to generate solutions. As an electrical contractor and power generation company with 3 departments in Generator sales, Generator service, and Electrical Contracting, we have a variety of different ways to affect the lives of our customers and clients, which is what makes my role so fulfilling.

As my background is not in the electrical trade, my contribution to the company was not going to be primarily through my knowledge of the trade. However, what my lack of knowledge of the trade has enabled me to do is to stay focused on the people on the team. Two examples of things I teach my team:'

1. Always let the customer be in control of the decision, don't ever take that from them. Give them as much information as they need to make an informed decision but allow them to own the decision. The respect that you show in this engagement will keep us humble and keep customers returning as friends.

2. In any organization with motivated team members, where there are various levels of responsibility and skill, it's often a motivating factor for the team to know what the next potential steps are in their career path. And one of the most important steps for me in identifying that next leader is when a person develops the attitude and ability to assist other teammates and customers with no regard for their own position. A great teammate is focused on the goal and not solely focused on their own self.

The four attributes that describe the Power Connection in a word are: Dependable, Good Teammate, Character/trustworthy, and Driven. These attributes are the values that the TPC team has identified best describe who we are. Our company has been transformed over the last several months by consistently communicating the Mission, Vision, and Values to the team.

How does this translate to our customers?

One of the most significant ways that TPC has been impacted is that the hurdles of growing the company by about 50% in the span of 4 months, is that the team has a common base from which to work through the many challenges that we have faced in this growth. Great attitudes, positive energy, and the solutions generated, result in efficient projects, and positive experiences for our clients. We have realized financial savings, and time efficiencies that have been critical to making projects successful for our partners.

It has taken about 10 years, but when the values that the company was based on have started to take hold and the majority of the team shares similar values, Challenges become opportunities, breakeven projects become money makers, customers become Fans, and dearest to my heart, EMPLOYEES become PARTNERS!

Jordan Rohrer
President
The Power Connection

Neighbors Serving Neighbors: How an 84-Year-Old Cooperative Turned Five Values into a Way of Life

As General Manager of our Cooperative, it is my duty to ensure that our values are recognized by ALL who come into contact with our business. This includes employees and clients. Since 1942, Rockingham Petroleum Cooperative has kept its word by weaving five core values—Integrity, Service, Community, Safety, and Stewardship—into every tank, every invoice, and every conversation.

Integrity is not a poster in the lobby; it is the reason a client can call and get transparent answers about our products and services. When crude markets gyrate, we absorb volatility when we can and explain it plainly when we cannot. We do not like hidden fees with vendors we utilize and have found our clients do not like them as well. We truly treat everyone the way we wish to be treated in return. That honesty has compounded for over eight decades.

Service, around here, is personal. Our employees grew up on these back roads in our area; many still farm on the weekends. "Neighbors Serving Neighbors" is a motto that we live by every day. It's often said around the office that "Our best is the least can do". Service is what has enabled us to stay in business through the years.

Community is ownership—literal ownership. Every gallon a member buys earns equity. Over the past ten years we have returned more than fifteen million dollars in patronage checks. Those checks allow our members to reinvest that equity back into their home operations. It also means we support each other in the community. The Cooperative is not a charity; it is a circle. Whether it is buying a 4-H animal at the county fair, helping sponsor a championship little league team, or providing hazardous material response training to local fire departments. Money spent here stays here, and the circle keeps turning.

Safety is non-negotiable. We train harder, inspect more often, and replace equipment sooner than regulations demand. We would rather lose a day's revenue than risk one life. That discipline has given us one of the lowest incident rates in our region, and it lets families sleep easy knowing the tank in their backyard is watched over like our own.

Stewardship means planning for grandchildren we haven't met yet. We offer the highest quality, most efficient energy products available to consumers today. We use proprietary additives in many of our products to ensure cleaner combustion, keeping emissions at the lowest possible levels. Every choice asks the same question: Does this leave the land, the co-op, and the community stronger tomorrow than it is today?

These values do not sit in separate silos; they lean against one another like beams in an old barn. Integrity makes flexible payment plans possible when a harvest fails. Safety creates the skilled workforce that keeps furnaces alive longer, saving fuel and money. Community investment produces the stable rural economy that still supports family farms—and family farms are the reason this cooperative exists at all.

After eight-four years, the tankers are shinier, the computers faster, and the fuels cleaner, but the promise is unchanged: when you call

Rockingham Petroleum, someone local answers, someone who knows your road and your story. We not only have a mission and a vision, we have a way of life.

Josh Stephens
General Manager
Rockingham Petroleum Cooperative

WORKS CITED

Chapter One

1 Dove, Wes. *Leading With a Clear Purpose: Steps Every Leader Should Take to Define Their Own and Provide One for Everyone on Their Team!* Dove Development & Consulting Press, 2025.

2 Dove, Wes. *What's KILLING Your Profitability? (It ALL Boils Down to Leadership!).* Dove Development & Consulting Press, 2024.

3 Maxwell, John C. There's No Such Thing as "Business" Ethics: There's Only One Rule for Making Decisions. New York: Warner Books, 2003.

4 U.S. Bureau of Labor Statistics. "Job Openings and Labor Turnover Summary." United States Department of Labor, 30 Sept. 2025, www.bls.gov/news.release/jolts.nr0.htm.

Chapter Two

5 Steinhorst, Curt. "Rethinking the Value of Core Values." *Forbes*, October 17, 2019. https://www.forbes.com/sites/curtsteinhorst/2019/10/17/rethinking-the-value-of-core-values/.

6 Lencioni, Patrick M. "Make Your Values Mean Something." *Harvard Business Review*, July–August 2002. https://hbr.org/2002/07/make-your-values-mean-something.

7 Sull, Donald, Stefano Turconi, and Charles Sull. "When It Comes to Culture, Does Your Company Walk the Talk?" *MIT Sloan Management Review*, July 21, 2020. https://sloanreview.mit.edu/article/when-it-comes-to-culture-does-your-company-walk-the-talk/.

8 Federal Bureau of Investigation. "Enron Code of Ethics." Last modified December 21, 2022. https://www.fbi.gov/history/artifacts/enron-code-of-ethics.

9 Sacramento State University. "Statement on Human Rights Principles." California State University, Sacramento. Accessed October 21, 2025. https://www.csus.edu/umanual/hr/hrs-0116.html.

Chapter Three

10 "The Impact of Organizational Ambiguity on Performance Evaluation Metrics." Vorecol Blog, September 17, 2024. https://vorecol.com/blogs/blog-the-impact-of-organizational-ambiguity-on-performance-evaluation-metrics-190808.

11 Shaw, George Bernard. *Man and Superman: A Comedy and a Philosophy*. London: A. Constable, 1903.

12 "Why Ambiguity Leads to Lower Work Performance." meQuilibrium, October 15, 2020. https://www.mequilibrium.com/resources/why-ambiguity-leads-to-lower-workforce-performance/.

13 Henderson, Jeff. *Know What You're FOR: A Growth Strategy for Work, an Even Better Strategy for Life*. Grand Rapids: Zondervan, 2016.

14 Maxwell, John C. *The 15 Invaluable Laws of Growth: Live Them and Reach Your Potential*. New York: Center Street, 2012.

Chapter Four

15 Levin, Marissa. "9 Ways to Reinforce and Live Your Company's Core Values Every Day." Inc., May 31, 2017. https://www.inc.com/marissa-levin/9-ways-to-reinforce-and-live-your-companys-core-values-every-day.html.

16 Buchanan, Leigh. "The Things They Do for Love." Harvard Business Review, December 2004. https://hbr.org/2004/12/the-things-they-do-for-love.

17 Lesley University. "The Power of Company Core Values." Accessed October 21, 2025. https://lesley.edu/article/the-power-of-company-core-values.

18 Pink, Daniel H. When: The Scientific Secrets of Perfect Timing. New York: Riverhead Books, 2018.

Chapter Five

19 CX Today. "McDonald's Is Failing on Customer Satisfaction, Report Finds." May 29, 2024. https://www.cxtoday.com/crm/mcdonalds-is-failing-on-customer-satisfaction-report-finds/.

20 Wrigglesworth, Rachel. "The Poetry of Purpose: Inspirational Purpose Statement Examples." UseMotion, November 3, 2023. https://www.usemotion.com/blog/purpose-statement-examples.

Chapter Six

21 Steinhorst, Curt. "Rethinking the Value of Core Values." *Forbes*, October 17, 2019. https://www.forbes.com/sites/curtsteinhorst/2019/10/17/rethinking-the-value-of-core-values/.

22 Igniyte. "Workplace Culture and Its Impact on Corporate Reputation." Igniyte, August 14, 2024. https://www.igniyte.co.uk/blog/workplace-culture-and-its-impact-on-corporate-reputation/.

23 Sull, Donald, William R. Kerr, and Charles Sull. "When It Comes to Culture, Does Your Company Walk the Talk?" *MIT Sloan Management Review*, July 21, 2020. https://sloanreview.mit.edu/article/when-it-comes-to-culture-does-your-company-walk-the-talk/.

24 Maxwell, John C. *The 21 Irrefutable Laws of Leadership: Follow Them and People Will Follow You*. Nashville: Thomas Nelson, 1998.

25 *The Holy Bible: New Living Translation*. Wheaton, IL: Tyndale House Publishers, 1996.

Chapter Seven

26 Sameer Building Construction. "How Deep Are the Foundations of a Skyscraper?" Accessed October 21, 2025. https://sameerabuildingconstruction.com/how-deep-are-the-foundations-of-a-skyscraper/.

27 Baldwin, Kai. "Hoover Dam Construction | Overview, History & Purpose." Study.com. Updated November 21, 2023. https://study.com/academy/lesson/the-construction-of-the-hoover-dam-history-of-events.html.

28 Frost, Robert. 1915. "The Road Not Taken." In Mountain Interval, 1. New York: Henry Holt and Company.

29 *The Holy Bible: New Living Translation*. Wheaton, IL: Tyndale House Publishers, 1996.

30 Maxwell, John C. *Everyone Communicates, Few Connect: What the Most Effective People Do Differently*. Nashville: Thomas Nelson, 2010.

Chapter Eight

31 Google. "AI Overview for 'mission, vision, culture, values'." Generated October 21, 2025. https://www.google.com/search?q=mission%2C+vision%2C+culture%2C+values.

32 Juetten, Mary. "Leadership Tips: Setting the Example." *Forbes*, August 22, 2019. https://www.forbes.com/sites/maryjuetten/2019/08/22/leadership-tips-setting-the-example/.

33 Maxwell, John C. *The 17 Indisputable Laws of Teamwork: Embrace Them and Empower Your Team*. Nashville: Thomas Nelson, 2001.

34 Gibbons, Barry J. *This Indecision is Final: 32 Management Secrets of Albert Einstein, Billie Holiday, and a Bunch of Other People Who Never Worked 9 to 5*. Chicago: Dearborn Trade Publishing, 1996.

35 Wickman, Gino. Traction: Get a Grip on Your Business. Dallas: BenBella Books, 2011.

Chapter Ten

36 Maxwell, John C. *The 21 Irrefutable Laws of Leadership: Follow Them and People Will Follow You*. Nashville: Thomas Nelson, 1998.

37 Maxwell, John C. *The 15 Invaluable Laws of Growth: Live Them and Reach Your Potential*. New York: Center Street, 2012.

38 Gibbs, Joe. *Racing to Win: Establish Your Game Plan for Success*. Sisters, OR: Multnomah Publishers, 2002.

39 Cathy, S. Truett. *Eat Mor Chikin: Inspire More People*. Decatur, GA: Looking Glass Books, 2002.

Chapter Eleven

40 Henderson, Jeff. *Know What You're FOR: A Growth Strategy for Work, an Even Better Strategy for Life*. Grand Rapids: Zondervan, 2016.

41 Sull, Donald, William R. Kerr, and Charles Sull. "When It Comes to Culture, Does Your Company Walk the Talk?" *MIT Sloan Management Review*, July 21, 2020. https://sloanreview.mit.edu/article/when-it-comes-to-culture-does-your-company-walk-the-talk/.

42 Vaynerchuk, Gary. *Day Trading Attention: How to Actually Build Brand and Sales in the New Social Media World*. New York: Harper Business, 2024.

43 Wickman, Gino. *Traction: Get a Grip on Your Business*. Dallas: BenBella Books, 2011.

MEET THE AUTHOR

Wes Dove founded Dove Development & Consulting in 2015 to help organizations improve their profitability by building better leaders. Previously, Wes did extensive work in behavior-based safety throughout North America. He studied Human Resource Management at Columbia Southern University and holds a professional certification in human resources through the Society of Human Resource Management (SHRM-CP) with over 25 years of experience in safety, human resources, and personnel development in manufacturing, mining, and construction. He published the Amazon #1 Best-Seller, *What's KILLING Your Profitability? (It ALL Boils Down to Leadership!)*, in 2024. In February 2025, Dove published *Leading With A Clear Purpose*, a second Amazon #1 Best-Seller. He was also a contributing author to two other prior titles.

You can learn more at dove-development.net or contact him directly at wes@dove-development.net

Join *The Values Advantage* community, complete the diagnostic, and learn how you can access *The Values Advantage FRAMEWORK* for your organization at www.tva-advantage.com